[Reaching] your K i DS

KaREN DOCKReY

a TeAM STRaTEGY for PaRENTS
and YOuTH WoRKERs

[Reaching] your

KiDS

KaREN DOCKReY

BROADMAN
&HOLMAN
PUBLISHERS

NaSHViLLE, TeNNESsEE

0-8054-24849

Published by Broadman & Holman Publishers
Nashville, Tennessee

Dewey Decimal Classification: 268
Subject Heading: RELATIONSHIPS/PARENTING

Scripture quotations are from the Holy Bible, New International Version,
©copyright 1973, 1978, 1984 by the International Bible Society.

1 2 3 4 5 6 7 8 9 10 06 05 04 03 02

Six Parent Ministry Approaches For Each of Ten Themes

You've committed to minister to parents as well as teenagers, but after a full week of contacting, teaching, and loving youth, you have no time left to give the parents. What do you do?

Schedule meetings? Yes and no. This resource offers ten complete meetings with pithy content blended throughout. But because not all parents can get to meetings and because no youth minister can hold a meeting for every issue that arises, the book also includes five other ministry approaches for each of the ten themes. The six approaches in each chapter are:

1. *Parent workshop*—This is the main portion of the chapter. It equips you to lead a parent workshop or adapt it for a youth-parent meeting if youth will be present. Each parent workshop provides a goal, content blended with teaching approaches, step-by-step lists of supplies and preparations, and a closing point parents can take home. Most include more ideas than you can use in an hour, and you can supplement with content from the other five sections.

2. *Home discussion guides*—Send a discussion guide home with parents after the meeting, or mail it to each parent a few days after the session as a follow-up prompter to practice the point of the session. You might also mail it during a month you don't have a parent meeting, or use it as an outreach to parents who could not attend the workshop.

3. *Newsletter ideas*—Use or adapt these ideas to fit the space you have in a parent newsletter or as part of the all-church newsletter. Youth might want to use these ideas as a starting ground for writing their own articles to parents.

4. *E-mail ideas*—In addition to sending newsletters, try these brief parent support ideas, tips, and strategies for the electronic medium. Some are short enough to send to cell phones or alphanumeric pagers.

5. *What teenagers want parents to know*—Ask your teens one or more of these questions to invite them to share anonymously with parents. The

goal is not to replace face-to-face communication but to provide supplementary opportunity for parents to see things from a teen point of view. Use this positively and sensitively. Feel free to choose one question at a time as the "Question of the Week."

6. *Troubleshooting*—Parenting seldom happens like solving a clean algebra problem. It takes tons of persistence. Here are tips to help parents keep on keeping on.

Bonus Ideas

In addition to these every-chapter elements, you'll find a bonus idea that works particularly well with each chapter theme. These are:

Chapter 1: How to Guide without Nagging—This list of tips will help parents monitor their teens' behavior well without their teens feeling like parents are on their case (well OK, they might still feel like you're on their case, but you'll know you aren't).

Chapter 2: This Family Fights Well—This refrigerator display shows parents and teens how to talk through problems without fighting.

Chapter 3: Let God Check You—This reproducible prayer guide can be used weekly to keep communication flowing well between teens and parents.

Chapter 4: Sample Paths Toward Independence—Because independence is a process, this list offers sample strategies for specific areas of independence. Parents can add others custom-designed for their teenagers.

Chapter 5: Making Work Fun—Because work is much more than a way to earn money, this guide shows parents and teens how to minister through their jobs, even when those jobs are as simple as bagging groceries.

Chapter 6: A Dozen Blessings to Give Your Teen—Because genuine blessings from parents give teens the power to love others in godly ways, provide these starter ideas to jump-start the blessing process.

Chapter 7: Guide Your Teen to Be a Good Date—Because teens aren't born knowing how to meet and charm dates, this guide gives parents fodder for teaching their teens how to delight, and delight in, the opposite sex.

Chapter 8: Haven Magnet—Because both teens and parents want a home that's a haven, guide parents to post this magnet on their refrigerator.

Chapter 9: Temptation Is No Puzzle—Though temptation can be confusing, there are at least four no-brainer solutions to it. Challenge teens and their parents to find these with this puzzle and then to practice them.

Chapter 10: Places to Go for Answers—To guide your teenagers to ask, seek, and knock, print this trifold card to keep in teen and parent billfolds.

Ten Commandments of Parent Ministry

1. *You will never have enough time to do parent ministry.* So just start. The old adage "something is better than nothing" applies here. Go ahead and put quarterly meetings on the calendar, link them to a time parents are already at church (such as following Sunday morning worship), and get rolling.

2. *Communicate with more than just meetings.* Most parents are not apathetic. They simply have too much to do. Their teens are also a bit uneasy with parents "getting together to talk to other parents about me." So use newsletters (ideas enclosed), home discussion sheets (privacy provided), E-mail prompters (light a fire; don't condemn), even cell phone pages. Each will contribute to the effectiveness of the other.

3. *Refuse to allow "my teen is worse than your teen" talk.* The best way to avoid a teen's fear of "getting together to talk about me" is to not do it. Squash parental whining, complaining, and one-upping. Too many parents want to wear teenager-trouble as a badge of honor. Stop this worldly and totally unproductive process. It simply gives parents an excuse not to act.

4. *Communicate a "we're just a little further along" stance.* Teenagers don't win the prize for moodiness, impulsiveness, laziness, and failing to think about the effects of their actions. There are plenty of adults who display these same behaviors. Replace "teenagers are trouble" myths with "everybody has good and bad days" and "it's our job as parents to guide teens to create good days." Stress that we adults are just a bit further along in the eternal scheme of things.

5. *Intentionally motivate a "teens are wonderful" approach.* Teens *do* have heightened emotions; teens *do* have much to learn about how to take on

life as an adult. But teens are also deeply compassionate, passionately idealistic, and absolutely convinced that this world would become perfect if people just lived according to God's guidance. Urge parents to tap into teens' good qualities, while guiding them toward the next step of maturity.

6. *Remember that changes don't happen automatically.* Parents must teach, train, discipline, reward, and supervise their teens if they want their teens to turn out all right. Even more difficult, they must be consistent and persistent. Being a Christian does not take away these God-given responsibilities; it heightens them.

7. *Replace rumors with facts.* Parents are still important in teen lives. Parents can make their teenagers behave. Teenagers crave rules and the secure love that comes through them. Parents can't choose these realities, but they can choose whether they will neglect their teenagers or go ahead and persistently guide them to goodness.

8. *Combine your efforts with those of parents to meet the needs of youth.* Youth ministers don't have all the answers, but they do have some. Parents know their teenagers best and have the greatest impact on those teenagers, but they want to learn how their teens act when parents are not around. So combine your efforts, learn from each other, and enhance the actions of the other. Listen to parental wisdom while sharing your ideas. Share your wisdom while listening to parental ideas. As youth workers and parents steer teenagers together, they more effectively compel youth to "act justly and to love mercy and to walk humbly with" God (Mic. 6:8).

9. *Invite teenagers to your meetings at least occasionally.* Through parents meeting other teens, and teens meeting other parents, all discover that their families are not so strange after all. Each learns that each has much to give and much to learn from the others. The *Adaptation for a Youth-Parent Meeting* tips in each chapter show you how.

10. *Involve parents in your ministry decision making.* Parents who know their teens bring a critical perspective to mission trip planning, programming, and more. Let your cooperation be truly two-way, letting parents help you with youth ministry while you help them with parenting.

And finally, a bonus command that surrounds all of the above: Challenge adults to bring their own Bibles to parenting meetings. God, not creative lessons, is the power source for effective parenting. So guide parents (and yourself) to know God through His Word. As they learn from and mark the Bible they take home, they are more likely to find and live those verses during the week.

Bonus Chapters

Check out the three mini-chapters at the back of this book for a parent ministry strategy, a guide for writing your own parent workshop session, and more than four dozen theme ideas.

Features

Each full-length chapter includes these features, and more:

Fully integrated—The content is woven with the teaching plan. This keeps you from having to blend content and method yourself, while still allowing you freedom to custom design the session for your group of parents.

Super-easy to prepare—Each step tells exactly what supplies you need and what preparation to make. Copy set in bold indicates suggested words for the leader to say. Bulleted lists set in italics indicate possible answers to use to start discussions or to continue if talk slows.

Respects the wisdom of parents—Rather than saddle the youth minister with the ridiculous assumption that the youth minister knows all there is to know about parenting, this book enables you to be a catalyst for the massive parental wisdom in your church. Some will know (and practice) more than others, but all will know more than any one individual.

Consistent, yet unique—Though the same features appear in each session, each session is unique in flow, in approach, in teaching methods, and more. Parents won't have the sense of "we've done this before" as they attend several sessions.

Stands alone or supports a series—You can use a single parent meeting or all ten of them. Each stands alone, and each can support the others.

Flexible—You can pull from the Home Discussion Guides and Newsletter Ideas to supplement your meetings. You can draw more newsletter and home discussion ideas from the sessions.

Full of tips—In each chapter you'll find these tips, signaled by their own icons:

▶ The Point

To make certain you get the main point across, send home this ready-to-reproduce point.

Teaching Tip

No matter how experienced you are, the way you teach is as important as what you teach. This tip is custom designed for the session in which it appears.

Time Note

Your time may run short or long. You may have parents who talk more or less than expected. This tip will help you over those bumps.

Adaptation for a Youth-Parent Meeting

If youth are present, invite them not only to participate in all steps but also to participate in these ways.

A Few More Ideas on Using This Book

1. Need to write an article for this week's newsletter? It's here.

2. Want to send a quick E-mail of encouragement on a topic your parents have asked about? That's here too.

3. Wish you could draw the wisdom of all your parents together and distribute it? The ten complete programs help this happen.

4. Did the last parent session you led become a "What do you think?" pooling of ignorance because you didn't have time to research? Meaty content is woven into each teaching plan to give substance to every bite.

5. Are your teens on a soapbox wishing their parents would listen? You'll find questions and venues through which teens can share their "wish you knew this" with parents.

6. Don't have time for another meeting right now but want to equip in a specific skill? Home discussion guides equip parents when you physically can't.

7. Worried that you bumbled the last meeting and didn't get the point across? Send home the ready-to-reproduce point.

Contents

"I will instruct you and teach you in the way you should go; I will counsel you and watch over you. Do not be like the horse or the mule, which have no understanding but must be controlled by bit and bridle."

(Ps. 32:8–9)

1. I Can't Make My Teen Do Anything   1

Oh yes, you can; the teen years are perhaps the most critical years for discipline.

Remembering that the root of discipline is "disciple," match enjoyments and privileges to teen behaviors to guide your teens to become all God wants them to be (Ps. 32:8–9).

2. We Fight Too Much   22

So communicate instead.

By calmly but firmly showing your teen what to do and why to do it, and then insisting that your teen choose well, there will be less fighting in your home (Gal. 5:15).

3. My Teenager Just Hides in Her Room   39

So bring her out.

Establish and keep daily contact with your teenagers. In so doing your teen will learn to talk through both easy and hard times (Prov. 17:27).

4. My Teen Doesn't Want to Be Seen with Me in Public   56

So show your teen how to be independent.

Your teen's hesitance is based on a need to be known and seen as competent. Because nobody's born knowing how to do independence well, give your teens increasing responsibilities and show them how to manage those responsibilities (Deut. 6:6–7).

5. My Teenager Thinks I'm Made of Money   73

So demonstrate how work brings freedom.

Give your teen increasing accountability to earn and manage his or her own money. Show your teen how to balance money-earning with church involvement. Warn your teen against money-traps such as greed, status, and letting things own them. In all these ways your teen will find true freedom (Phil. 4:11–12).

6. My Teenager Doesn't Like Himself   95

So like him boldly until he can act with competence and confidence.
Encourage with your words; then validate your words with your
actions to spur your teen on to the competent and caring actions that
feed true confidence (Heb. 10:24–25).

7. They're Getting Too Serious   117

So protect them emotionally, sexually, and spiritually.
Guide your teenagers to notice and go after qualities of godliness in
their guy/girl relationships, while they develop those qualities in themselves (Gal. 5:22–23).

8. My Teen Is Under So Much Pressure   138

So reinforce your teen to manage it.
Show your teen how to find power to do what is right and kind no matter how tired, how stressed, or how pressured he or she may be (Rom.
12:17, 21).

9. My Teen Didn't Mean to Give in to Temptation   157

*So armor your teen against the destroy-their-lives dangers that
lurk everywhere.*
Communicate fleeing as the most effective temptation-resisting strategy,
followed by deciding ahead of time what you will and won't do. Then
work together to learn and practice other strategies (1 Cor. 10:13).

10. My Teen Wonders If There's a God   176

So answer spiritual questions and mold spiritual habits.
Because God is the answer and generously shares answers, guide your
teenagers to search out and discover the answers to their spiritual
questions (Matt. 7:7).

BONUS 1: A Strategy for Ministering with Parents   197
A handful of ideas, cautions, and tips.

BONUS 2: Write Your Own Session   201
A sample process by which to compose a parent meeting on any topic.

BONUS 3: Over Four Dozen Topics for Parent Meetings   205
*Having trouble thinking of your next parent meeting or parent news-
letter theme? Try these.*

I Can't Make My Teen Do Anything

Oh yes, you can; the teen years are perhaps the most critical years for discipline.

"Once they get to seventh grade, they're beyond your control."

"You may be able to do a little in the seventh grade, but once they get their driver's license, you can no longer monitor teenage behavior."

These statements are simply not true. Quite contrary to popular opinion, teenagers deeply want and need their parents to continue to guide their lives. Study after study shows that teenagers crave time and conversation with their parents as well as limits and enforcement from their parents. Even when teens don't consciously crave guidance by parents, they need it. Teens rapidly lose respect for parents who ignore them or who give them too much freedom. In turn these teens test parents to see if anything will make them respond. When teenagers become sullen, rebel, or head toward risky behaviors, it's time for parents to step up the involvement and intentionally steer behaviors back toward the healthy. When teenagers are happy, cooperative, and choosing beneficial behaviors, it's time to keep up that contact and to reward that good behavior with a bit more freedom in the areas in which teens are doing well.

Parental influence is profound. The choice each parent makes is not whether to influence their teenagers but whether the influence they already have will be positive or negative. It's simply not true that parents are no longer relevant in their children's lives once they hit the magic age of thirteen.

Goal—This chapter guides parents to share strategies for steadily guiding their teenagers well.

PARENT WORKSHOP

Draw from these ideas to lead a one-hour parent workshop.

1. More Than a Game

You'll need a Bible, three-by-five-inch cards, pencils, masking tape, and markers. Write the four category posters with room to add suggestions around the category. Tear tape circles with which to hang up the posters. Arrange chairs in foursomes.

Option: Write the categories on computer-generated cells to be projected on the wall; include space for answers.

As parents enter, gather them in teams of three to five by pointing them to chairs set up in circles. When one circle fills up, start another group. As each group fills, point out to that group Poster 1, which you have displayed on the wall with masking tape (the other three category posters are hidden for now). Give the group a three-by-five-inch card and a pencil with which to write their answers.

Poster 1: Write six things teenagers enjoy doing when no one is telling them what to do.

Keep forming teams until starting time or until all parents have arrived, prompting them to write more than six things if they have time. *Samples, not to be written on the poster, but for you to use to jump-start groups:*
- *Spend time with friends.*
- *Talk on phone.*
- *Talk on-line.*
- *Use the computer.*
- *Paint.*
- *Listen to music.*
- *Work on cars.*
- *Watch television.*
- *Play sports.*
- *Go out.*

Begin the game by calling for each team to name one item on its list of six. If no one else has listed that item, they circle it on their cards. If anyone else has it, all teams cross it off. The process is similar to Scattergories,® available in discount department stores and in toy stores.

Say: **The purpose of this game is to look for unique answers. We'll keep a record of all answers, even repeated ones, by writing each on the category poster.**

Consider enlisting a parent to be the scribe for this process.

Say: **Parenting teenagers is no game, but it can be loads of fun. We are playing a game that accomplishes three parenting purposes: (1) It gets us comfortable talking together so we can share parenting ideas. (2) It helps us list characteristics of teenagers that we'll use later to understand how to love our teens better. (3) It demonstrates that blending wisdom to solve a problem can be both fun and positive. Let's continue with the next category, following the same process. One extra rule: Talk positively about your teens rather than tell bad stories about them. You can do this by talking in generalities.** Write this rule on a poster or chalkboard.

Do the listing and reporting the same way for the next three posters, except start with a different team and report in another sequence (e.g., instead of going left around the circle, go right around the circle this time). Change the starter team and the order of the teams for each round. Reveal one poster at a time as you play. Remember to write ALL suggestions on the topic poster that matches it. Use generous affirmation so parents will feel comfortable contributing. The other categories:

Poster 2: Write six privileges from which teenagers profit or would like to profit.

Samples, not to be written on the poster, but for you to use to jump-start groups:
- *Drive a car.*
- *Stay up late.*
- *Choose when to do homework.*
- *Spend money.*
- *Use a cell phone.*
- *Go out on weekends.*
- *Go out on a weeknight.*
- *Have a private room at home.*

Poster 3: List six actions you want your teenager to express as a responsible adult.

Samples, not to be written on the poster, but for you to use to jump-start groups:

- *Become a Christian.*
- *Live as a Christian.*
- *Live lovingly with family and friends.*
- *Pay own expenses.*
- *Pick up room.*
- *Do chores cheerfully.*
- *Finish homework.*
- *Choose caring words.*
- *Take turns.*
- *Tell the truth.*
- *Obey the Bible.*
- *Care about the impact of their actions.*

Poster 4: List six habits you want your teenager to stop by the time he or she becomes an adult.

Samples, not to be written on the poster, but for you to use to jump-start groups:

- *Talking ugly about people.*
- *Picking bad friends.*
- *Gossiping.*
- *Making excuses.*
- *Skipping school.*
- *Giving in to every emotion.*
- *Sleeping so late.*
- *Criticizing his brother.*
- *Crashing cars.*
- *Spending my money.*

Say: **You are brilliant parents. You have listed a total of _____ ideas** *(add all ideas from all four posters)* **for parenting teenagers well. Too often parents say, "I can't make my teenager do anything." They believe the rumor that once teens get to the seventh grade, or get their driver's licenses, there's nothing they can do to guide them. But this is simply not** true. You have shown that there are many ways to guide our teens and many reasons to guide your teen. You may not realize you listed ways to guide teens, but when you pair enjoyments and privileges *(point to the first two posters)*, with behaviors to start and stop *(point to the second two posters)*, you find effective parenting strategies.

Invite a parent volunteer to read Psalm 32:8 as God's promise to guide us.

Say: **Because God will guide you, you can legitimately guide your teens toward being the people God wants them to be. Let's find out how to put these together.** *(Point out all four posters.)*

Teaching Tip

If your goal for this step is to get a poster filled with ideas, why not just have parents call out ideas? Why bother with the game? Because only a few will talk if you have parents call out ideas. The smaller groups give every parent opportunity to participate. It also gives a little more privacy/anonymity to the answer. The competition adds the kind of healthy laughter that takes away the self-consciousness of talking about parenting. You'll not only get more answers; you'll also get fewer canned answers and a greater variety of answers.

Adaptation For a Youth-Parent Meeting

If youth are present, invite them to write on three-by-five-inch cards why they want their parents involved in their lives. Assure them before they write that you and you alone will read these cards and that you will read them aloud for this meeting, but you won't identify who wrote what. Make certain all teens write in pencil. Read these cards after step 1.

2. How They Match Up

You'll need the four filled-in posters from step 1.

Say: **Disciplining teens makes many parents bristle. What's the first word or feeling that comes to your mind when you think about disciplining your teen?**

Direct parents to call out the answers popcorn style without comment. Expect a wide variety, depending on parenting style, age of teens, and skills already learned.

Samples include:
- *Process*
- *Scary*
- *Adventure*
- *New*
- *Creative*
- *Punish*
- *Changing*
- *Impossible*
- *Consequences*
- *Possible*
- *Hopeful*
- *Fearful*
- *Hard*
- *Joy*
- *Ineffective*
- *Loving*

The word *discipline* comes from the same root as the word *disciple*. Our goal in discipline is not to punish, but to guide our teens toward Christlikeness.

To begin practicing how to guide our teens to Christlike behavior, call for volunteers to find a behavior on Poster 3 (actions you want your teenager to express as a responsible adult) and to pick an enjoyment or privilege from the first two posters that would be like a carrot on a stick to get teens to do that responsible behavior. For example, a parent who chose "do chores cheerfully" might choose:

- You may talk on the phone as soon as you finish your chore.
- You may get on the computer if you do your chore cheerfully. But if you gripe, you can't get on the computer today or tomorrow either. (For the savvy teen who says, "I'll just gripe and wait two days; at least I won't have to do the chore," parents could add: no matter how many days it takes you, you must do your chore before getting on the computer again.)
- Because it's more fun to whistle while you work, you may listen to music while you do your chore. But if you complain, we turn off the music.

- As soon as you finish the chore cheerfully, you may leave to meet your friends.
- You may drive the car as long as you keep it vacuumed. If you don't vacuum it thoroughly by Thursday, you can't use it on the weekend.
- If you do your chores cheerfully Monday through Friday, you may stay up as late as you want on Friday. Otherwise, you go to bed thirty minutes earlier than 10 P.M. for each day you grouse.

After each volunteer makes a match, cite something wise about what they said such as: **That reward will make your teenager want to speak cheerfully.** Or, **If teenagers could raise themselves, they wouldn't need us to show them how to live in ways that honor God.**

Then invite several different volunteers to name a behavior they want to stop from Poster 4 and name an enjoyment or privilege from the first two posters they could withdraw as a motivation to stop that behavior. For example, a parent who chose "picking bad friends" might choose two of these consequences:

- Because I want you to be happy, I want you to choose good friends. You'll earn privileges for choosing good friends, and you'll lose privileges for spending time with not-so-good friends.
- If you bring the friends here first so I can meet and know them, you will have the privilege of driving the car to their homes. If you don't bring them here first, you can't drive to their homes.
- If I find that you have spent time with negative friends anyway, you will lose driving privileges for at least a full week. I'll drive you to school, to church, to friends' homes, on dates, everywhere you go.
- If I don't have a phone number for the parent in the home for any party you attend, you will not go to that party.
- If you choose to call *(name of bad friend)*, I'll choose to withdraw your cell phone and your home phone privileges.
- You may chat via computer, but I must be in the room and know the person with whom you're chatting. If you chat without me, you won't chat for a month.

Again, affirm each contribution.

Say: **We really can legislate morality, can't we? Every traffic ticket and every stop sign helps us take care of the people in the other cars. In the same way—every withdrawn privilege or provided pleasure makes teens want to avoid cruel or irresponsible behaviors and choose caring or happy behaviors.**

The key to being a good parent to our teenagers is to match the enjoyments and privileges to the behaviors that match godliness. You've named ways to hold a carrot of reward in front of your teens to motivate them to do the right thing, and you've named ways to withdraw privileges to stop not-so-right things. How are these processes similar to the ways God guides us?

Samples:

- *God gives us the Ten Commandments and then shows why they work.*
- *God guides us until we understand the principle and can choose it for ourselves; that's the relationship between law-motivation and heart-motivation.*
- *God expects us to obey Him all the time.*
- *God loves us and wants us to be happy.*
- *God knows more than we do and shares His wisdom with us.*
- *God lets us experience the consequences of our behavior, both good and bad.*
- *God walks right beside us to let us know we are not alone.*

After several comments, continue this discussion with questions like:

- **What's the difference between the privilege/reward matching process and controlling our teenagers?** *As parents answer, stress that control is for our sakes, and guidance is for teens' sakes. Also stress that God will guide us so we can guide our teenagers. As we imitate God's guidance, we will be better parents.*
- **What's the difference between this process and being mean?** *While parents respond, point out that even if our teens think we're mean, good parenting acts with an eye toward good.*
- **How can we make certain we are imitating God rather than controlling our teens or acting cruelly toward them?** *(Samples: Get someone to watch us; check our motivations; watch our own moods; realize that teens will call us mean and controlling even when we're not, just to get out of whatever the directive is.)*

3. The Impact I'll Have

You'll need a poster and a marker board or computer-generated display to record answers. Write on your poster or marker board the fill-in-the-blank sentence.

Say: **For better or for worse, your influence as a parent is profound. It's simply not true that parents are no longer relevant in their children's lives once they hit the magic age of thirteen. Contrary to popular opinion, studies show that teenagers deeply want and need their parents to continue to guide their lives. We definitely influence our teenagers; we just need to decide whether that influence will be positive or negative. Let's dream about this for a moment.**

Invite each parent to name a positive impact they want to have on their teenagers and what might bring about that impact, with none saying what another parent has said.

To help them know how to say this, write this fill-in-the-blank sentence on the marker board:

I want my teen to _____ *as a result of* _____
_____.

Write all ideas on a large poster or use a laptop computer projected on a screen.

Samples:

- *I want my teens to choose right over wrong as a result of seeing me do that.*
- *I want my teen to enjoy the simple things as a result of our doing that as a family.*
- *I want my teens to be friends with their siblings as a result of our enforcing a "talk respectfully" rule.*
- *I want my teenagers to know God will always send a person to help as a result of their having experienced me being there for them.*
- *I want my teenagers to feel like adults as a result of my letting them take on adult responsibilities and experience both the easy and hard consequences of that.*
- *I want my teen to manage money well as a result of my showing them how to use a checkbook and refusing to bail them out.*

4. But It's Not That Easy

You'll need a timer. Duplicate and cut apart the eight sabotage slips. Make extras if you anticipate more than eight groups. Give each group more than one if you have less than eight groups.

Gather parents back into the teams they were in when they first arrived.

Say: **By letting God help us match results to behaviors, we parents have a positive influence on our teens' character. They respect us; we respect them; and, most important of all, they discover how God's world works. But matching these consequences and actually delivering them are two different things. I'm going to give each team a way to sabotage parental guidance. Plan to speak to the rest of us for forty-five seconds to explain why your sabotage stops the good parents try to do and how to overcome it. You'll have commentary on your slip, but feel free to modify or add to it.**

Give each team a sabotage slip. You may choose to cut off the discussion tips or leave them on to give the team more to draw on in their presentation. Suggest that each member of each team speak for about ten seconds. Positively tease and prompt them as they speak to make this easier for them to do. Time the groups with your watch.

Sabotage Slips

Sabotage 1: Wait until the action is over before you inform the teen of the consequences.

"Because you didn't finish the lawn, you can't go out." This reasonable consequence isn't fair if you didn't tell your teen beforehand that he had to finish the lawn before leaving. Let your teen know exactly what you expect and what will happen if that expectation is not fulfilled. The exception to the forewarning rule is a highly dangerous behavior that you were not able to anticipate, such as driving before the age of fifteen or saying something horribly ugly to a sibling. For such negative behaviors you must inflict consequences without advanced notice.

Sabotage 2: Use consequences for your benefit rather than your teenager's benefit.

You feel uneasy about the party your teen has been invited to attend, so you say you need him to baby-sit. You're relieved to have care for your younger children while you go out, but your son is furious. You would have had better success if you had explained your concerns about the party—that there are no adult chaperones, that you had watched the host use poor judgment in his driving and feared the same poor judgment in party giving. Then you and your teen could have negotiated another plan, such as a party at your house.

Sabotage 3: Be vague about expectations.

Remember that nobody's born knowing how. Your job as parent is to show your teen how to honor God with specific instruction followed by compassionate enforcement. Instead of "show a good attitude," say "show a good attitude by talking calmly when you're angry and talking kindly when you're stressed." Instead of "be mature" say, "I expect you to get along with your siblings on your own so I don't have to reprimand you." Teens can't do what they don't understand.

Sabotage 4: Change the rules.

If you said your teen could relax after doing chores, don't add another chore when your teen finishes. Instead, give a list at the beginning and stick to it. Certainly there are times when you must change the rules, such as falling and breaking your leg and needing your relaxing-after-chores teen to make supper while you're at the hospital, but make those instances so rare that your teen can trust your word.

Sabotage 5: Enforce the rule only occasionally.

If your teen knows there's a chance she can wiggle out of your expectation, she'll wiggle. She'll make an excuse, argue persistently, dawdle until you get tired of prodding, or do whatever it takes not to do what you said. But if you follow up what you say with consistency and calmness, she'll calmly and consistently do as you ask. A few up-front battles with staying firm no matter how much your teenager bucks will bring calmness in the long run.

Sabotage 6: Decide your teenager has too much stress to do the right thing.

Even when your teen has tons of homework, many church responsibilities, and several home chores, your teen can still follow the rules and do her part. Even when your teen comes home from the youth retreat absolutely exhausted, she can testify to God by being kind and getting along. Stress and fatigue are not excuses for grouchy or uncooperative behavior. They are times to call on God's supernatural power to help her choose patience, kindness, goodness, and self-control.

Sabotage 7: Attack your teenager.

Statements like "You can't do anything right!" "You'll never get into college with these grades!" and "I knew you'd never do it" diminish your teenager, not the irresponsible behavior. Instead, attack the problem: "I would guess you're disappointed about these grades too. Let's work out a study plan that will bring them up." Then work together to review the material, to make up silly memory tricks, to quiz together, to get tutoring, or to do whatever it takes to give your teen success with the subject. (WARNING: Grades do not define success; learning defines success.) Work together to create a good result after a frustrating problem.

Sabotage 8: Use only negative consequences.

The goal of good parenting is not to catch your teenager doing wrong; it's to guide your teen to choose self-discipline. Motivate your teen to choose behaviors by balancing rewards for good behavior with punishment for bad behavior. If you use too much of one or the other, your teenager will suffer. Too much reward encourages irresponsibility. Too much punishment destroys the confidence needed to choose the right thing.

After each less-than-a-minute speech, guide the parents to applaud.

Say: **We can continue to applaud one another in our parenting as we see other parents in the hallway, or as we E-mail, or as we talk on the phone.**

5. Dramatize the Dialogue

You'll need a chalkboard or marker board for the illustration. Write sample topics on three-by-five-inch cards to give to teams.

Say: **Teens rapidly lose respect for parents who ignore them or who give them too much freedom. In turn these teens test parents to see if anything will make them respond. When teenagers become sullen, rebel, or head toward risky behaviors, it's time to step up the involvement and intentionally steer behaviors back toward the healthy.**

As you say this write on the marker board the word *risky* and then draw about three stair steps up to the word *healthy.*

Say: **Sullen and unhappy teenagers are not the only ones who need guidance. When teenagers are happy, cooperative, and choosing beneficial behaviors, it's time to keep up that contact and to give a bit more freedom in the areas in which they're doing well.**

As you say this, write on the chalkboard three stair steps up to the words *even more beneficial.* Explain that many teens exhibit both negative and positive behaviors, sometimes in the same day. Whether the behavior is good or bad, our job as parents is to help our teens take a step up and a step forward each day. Stress that no matter how low our teens get, there is always a way to help them take higher steps. No matter how high they get, they can always use a word of encouragement and affirmation.

TIP: None of the above will do any good if you don't follow through with what you say. Actually monitoring to make certain your teen doesn't get on the computer when you said not to is both hard and easy. It's hard because it takes your energy and time, but it's easy because everyone's life gets easier when you do give truth to your word (your teen learns to heed your word, you can trust your teen, your teen shows good life habits, and so much more).

Time Note

> If time is almost over, stop the session here. The above stair-step illustration gives a good strong closure. But if you have time, the following discussion shows how to put the stair steps into action.

Guide parents to practice this through dramatizing conversations a parent might have with a teenager. One plays the teen, and the other plays the adult. Give a sample topic to each, and direct them to write and prepare to present a dialogue. For example, a parent whose teen needed to finish a scholarship application before Friday night might hold a conversation like this:

PARENT: I explained last Friday that you had to have that scholarship application finished before going to the ball game this Friday. You're not finished, so you'll have to stay in tonight and finish it.

TEEN: But Dad! It's homecoming! I can't miss this game!

PARENT: I wish you didn't have to miss it, but you chose not to get the application finished.

TEEN: I didn't choose. I was just busy.

PARENT: Choosing not to make time was choosing to not finish.

TEEN: But Dad, you know my week has been busier than usual. Can't you give me another week? I promise I'll do it TOMORROW if you just let me go to the game.

PARENT: Sorry. It has to be in the mail first thing tomorrow morning.

TEEN: Then I'll do it tonight when I come home. *Please,* Dad, you know how important this game is to me.

PARENT: And you knew you had to finish the scholarship application in time.

TEEN: You are TOTALLY unreasonable.

(Parent stays perfectly calm and explains that he can sit down and get at the scholarship application. If he finishes, and finishes well, he can go on to the game late. But he can do nothing else until the scholarship application is complete, checked, and is in the envelope.)

More sample topics:
- Guide a teen to manage a set amount of clothing money in preparation for supporting herself.
- Guide a teen to keep bedroom and bathroom neat.
- Get a teen to do chores cheerfully.
- Get a teen to do homework.
- Get a teen to talk kindly to siblings.
- Guide a teen to see the impact of actions.
- Equip a teen to manage emotions.
- Show a teen how to move past excuses to get done what needs to get done.

Write each of the above on three-by-five-inch cards and let each group choose the one they want. Offer the option of writing a situation of their own.

Adaptation for a Youth-Parent Meeting

If youth are present, invite them to play the role of parents, and parents to play the role of teens.

6. The Point

Make a copy of "The Point" on colorful paper to give to parents.

Instruct parents to think about times God has taught them something new, the tone with which He did this, and how they responded to God as one parent reads aloud Psalm 32:8–9. Encourage parents to guide their teens in imitation of the way God guides them. Give parents a copy of "The Point" printed on a wallet-sized card as they leave.

➤ The Point

Match enjoyments and privileges to teen behaviors to guide teens to become all God wants them to be.

"I will instruct you and teach you in the way you should go; I will counsel you and watch over you. Do not be like the horse or the mule, which have no understanding but must be controlled by bit and bridle" (Ps. 32:8–9).

Teens will be stubborn at first but eventually will choose the right ways with the same joy that God intends for us when He instructs us.

HOME DISCUSSION GUIDE

Send this page home with parents, mailing to any who were not able to attend, or mail to each parent a few days after the session as a follow-up prompter to practice the point.

The Point of our last parent meeting was to match enjoyments and privileges to teen behaviors to guide our teens to become all God wants them to be.

This point is based on the way God guides us: *"I will instruct you and teach you in the way you should go; I will counsel you and watch over you. Do not be like the horse or the mule, which have no understanding but must be controlled by bit and bridle"* (Ps. 32:8–9).

Three general approaches for doing this are:

1. Rewards
2. Adjusted privileges
3. Punishment

Cut the rewards, privileges, and punishments on page 17 apart and invite your teenager to stack them in order of preference, which would motivate him most to do the right thing for the right reason.

Communicate to your teens that you want to guide them to become Christlike and to take over their own discipline. The more good decisions they make for themselves, the less you will have to make for them. Then keep guiding. The rule of thumb is:

- Does this behavior make God's kingdom a better place?
- If so, affirm it. If not, motivate your teen to change it.

REWARD: Praise verbally: "Great job! I'm proud of you!"

REWARD: Increase privileges: "Because you drive carefully when I'm in the car and when neighbors see you, you may have the car tonight."

REWARD: Celebrate: "This report card is worth celebrating. You pick the restaurant!"

REWARD: Give gifts: "Because you've chosen music with good lyrics, I'd like to give you a new CD. Let's pick it together."

REWARD: Offer incentives: "You can gain more free time by hitting your homework hard so you complete it faster."

REWARD: Increase allowance: "If you do your chores without nagging, I'll give you a raise in January."

ADJUSTED PRIVILEGE: Carrot on a stick: "No phone talking or television until you finish your homework each day."

ADJUSTED PRIVILEGE: Give reasoned negotiations: "I can't let you drive your friends to the ball game because you got your license so recently. But you can choose one friend to ride with you if you let me approve him first."

PUNISHMENT: Fine: "If you leave your clothes on the floor, you'll pay me a dollar for every piece. I'll check every day at 6:00, and together we'll count the clothes."

ADJUSTED PRIVILEGE: It's your money: "I'll pay the price of generic blue jeans (or tennis shoes or whatever), and you make up the difference if you want that brand name."

ADJUSTED PRIVILEGE: Offer alternatives: "You can't buy or listen to that music. But I'll help you find a Christian band that plays similar music. As long as the lyrics and the lifestyle of the artist are good, you can play as wild a style as you want."

ADJUSTED PRIVILEGE: Blame the parent: "I realize you have mixed feelings about that event. So I'll give you the privilege of blaming me. Just be sure to tell me what I didn't let you do."

ADJUSTED PRIVILEGE: Take away: "Because you talked on-line rather than did your homework, you'll have no computer for a week." (HINT: Always match the punishment to the crime.)

PUNISHMENT: Allow consequences: "Because you got a speeding ticket, you'll have to pay it and the increased insurance costs."

PUNISHMENT: Administer consequences: "Because you lost your jacket, you'll earn the money to purchase a new one."

PUNISHMENT: Withhold privilege: "No driving until you pay off that speeding ticket."

PUNISHMENT: Impose extra labor: "Because you were cruel to your brother, you'll do his chores this week."

NEWSLETTER IDEA

Use these as a base for a parent newsletter, for youth-written articles, or for the parent section of the church newsletter.

Overcome the Myth

"Once they get to seventh grade, they're beyond your control." This is one of the devil's greatest tools for keeping teens off the right track. If teenagers were able to monitor their own lives, they would be out of your home, paying all their expenses, and participating as adults in the adult world. But they aren't. So they need you to guide them through the tricky time between childhood and adulthood. Here are five tips:

1. *Remember that* **discipline** *comes from the same root as* **disciple.** When parents continue to guide teenagers by enforcing rules for rightness, parents show teenagers how to be Christlike. For example: "Speak kindly to your brother, or you get to speak to no one by phone" teaches your teens how to love others as they love themselves.

2. *Recognize independence as a process, not a bestowal.* Independence doesn't mean dropping out of your teenagers' lives when they reach a certain age. Independence happens only as you show your teen how to manage each new freedom, one at a time.

3. *Yelling just makes everyone miserable.* Rather than complain about your teens, actually guide them. Replace, "You never pick up your room," with explaining that your teen can have free time as soon as her room is tidy. Calmly but persistently make sure the room is straight before she does any free-time activities (including dawdling in her room).

4. *Sullenness, rebellion, and failure are not normal teen behaviors.* Your teens can learn to manage their moods, express their disagreement healthily, show respect, express happiness, apply themselves, and be honest while doing these things. They'll need some consequences and a lot of teaching from you, but don't settle for anything less.

5. *The first few times you follow through, you may have to cancel your plans or stay up all night waiting, but then subsequent events will take less time.* Doing what you say you will do—making sure your teen actually finishes homework before going out—is the only way to raise teenagers well. You may have to cancel a night of your plans, but then

your teenagers will live in harmony with you and the world. Otherwise they buck you at every turn, and both of you stay miserable.

E-MAIL IDEAS

Choose from these parent support ideas, tips, and strategies especially for electronic transmission. (Remember: Don't create an E-mail Elite; print out and mail the messages to any parents who don't have E-mail).

Calling all strategies!

Dear Parents: Yelling and grounding are the two most frequently used strategies for getting our teens to do what they need to do, but they tend to be the least effective. Why? Teens can tune out yelling, and grounding seldom fits the crime. Will you E-mail back the strategies you find effective for guiding your teens toward daily goodness? We won't publish your name, just your idea. After gathering several, we'll send them back out to all of you for your parenting pleasure.

Here's one to get you thinking: "Trust is something you earn, not something that's bestowed on you at a certain age. So show me that you can stay kind and think clearly for a full week at that later bedtime, and I will trust your ability to pick that time as a good bedtime for you."

And if you're sending the E-mail to a cell phone, here's a short one: How are your actions today guiding your teen away from selfishness and toward Christlikeness?

WHAT TEENAGERS WANT PARENTS TO KNOW

Choose from these questions that invite your teens to share with you anonymous quotes, quips, and comments via E-mail or anonymous survey. Feel free to choose one question at a time as the "Question of the Week."

I'll combine your ideas with no names or identifying details to distribute to parents. Feel free to answer a question that's not here, or to suggest another question for everyone to answer:

- What's one really fair rule your parents have (even when you hate the rule, it's still a fair one)?

- What have you seen friends' parents do to raise your friends well?
- Why do you want to please your parents?
- What's a wimpy thing you've seen parents do (such as give in when they really should have stayed firm)?
- Why do you want your parents to stay involved in your life?

TROUBLESHOOTING

Suggest these actions to implement when a teen does not display the expected behavior.

Suppose you try to guide your teenager and your teen bucks rather than cooperates with you?

- Rejoice! Your teenager's job is to buck against your rules to see if those rules really matter enough to enforce.
- Insist that your teen do what you say. (God expects this from us.) Choice, not feeling, is the way to express love, joy, peace, patience, kindness, goodness, faithfulness, gentleness, self-control, and more (Gal. 5:22–23).
- Keep on insisting on right behavior for right reasons. It's a process that takes at least the six years of adolescence, in addition to the twelve you've already put in during childhood.

Bonus Idea

Follow the tips on the next page for monitoring without your teen feeling like you're on her case (well OK, she might still feel like you're on her case, but you'll know you aren't).

A sample way to use this idea is to enlarge it so it fits two to an 8½-by-11-inch sheet, each 4¼-by-11-inch, and suggest parents keep it on their bedroom mirror.

How to Guide without Nagging

1. Let your yes be yes, and your no be no (James 5:12).

2. Use calm action rather than agitated talk to make certain your teen behaves.

3. Explain your reasons.

4. Enforce your reasons even when your teen disagrees.

5. Be willing to be around so you can devise, advise, and supervise.

6. Catch your teen doing the right thing, and say what you see.

7. Let daily Christlike behavior be your goal.

CHAPTER 2

We Fight Too Much

So communicate instead.

"I'd discipline my teen, but I hate the fighting."

"Feelings just get in the way; my teen needs to do what I say. Doing the right thing, not feeling the right thing, is what matters."

Each of these extremes has a measure of truth. Disagreements can happen when parents guide teenagers down the right paths. And feelings aren't nearly as important as doing the right thing.

But fighting will be minimal with godly guidance. And we parents can blend understanding feelings with insistence on good behavior. In fact, our understanding is a critical element in the recipe for righteousness.

Do we just accept fighting as a given when we parent our teens? Not at all. Clear discussions, honorable disagreements, and harmonious living can become the rule rather than fighting in your home. This chapter shows you how. You will discover when to take a stand and when to negotiate. You will practice how to attack the problem without attacking each other. You can identify root causes of conflict so you know how to solve those causes. And you can separate healthy disagreement from dangerous conflict. Understanding will blend with action to provide calm guidance toward goodness.

Goal—This chapter guides parents to attack the problems rather than their teenagers. In so doing, parents leave fighting behind to discover more effective paths toward molding their teens.

PARENT WORKSHOP

Draw from these ideas to lead a one-hour parent workshop.

1. Don't Chop at the Foundation

You'll need Bibles and markers. Prepare a poster of a tree with enough roots for each parent. Make a paper hatchet. Arrange chairs in one large circle. Prepare duplicate posters and hatchets if you have more than ten parents.

As parents enter, give them a marker and direct them to the poster with an illustration of a tree with many roots going into the ground. You will have drawn this before class or enlisted an artistic parent or teen to do this ahead of time. (The concept is more critical than artistic perfection.) As parents enter, give each a marker and direct each to write on one root a foundation they want to give their teenagers, none repeating what another has written. To generate these ideas ask questions like:

Say: **From what roots do you want your teens' strength to come? How will you know your teens are well-grounded? What will make your teens strong? What life skills do you want your teens to have?**

Prepare duplicate posters if your group is larger than ten parents. *Sample foundations include:*

- *Security in Jesus*
- *Unending love from home*
- *Confidence to ask questions*
- *Ability to solve problems*
- *Good work ethic*
- *Excellent education*
- *Good relationship skills*
- *Enjoyment of simple things*
- *Joy*
- *Freedom to call parents for wisdom*
- *Connections to good people*
- *Wisdom in picking friends and a spouse*
- *Good friendships*

Congratulate parents for the godly foundations they want to build in their teenagers. Then draw or attach a hatchet labeled "FIGHTING" at the roots of the tree.

When we fight with our teenagers we cut at the very roots, the very foundations we're trying to build in their lives. Choosing not to fight does not mean giving in or avoiding conflict; it means to be the parent, to calmly and consistently lead. It means that you insist your teen do the right thing with all the loving action that God would give.

Invite a parent to read Ephesians 6:4. Point out that good guidance does not include exasperating your children.

2. Refuse to Pass on the Parenting

You'll need Bibles. Stuff a paper lunch sack with the sentence starters cut into strips. Prepare duplicate lunch sacks, and circles if you have more than ten parents.

Invite parents to clarify what it means to parent without fighting by passing a "hot bag" (a lunch sack twisted at the top and passed like a hot potato) around the circle. Whoever holds the bag when the music stops draws out one of the sentence starters and completes the sentence to clarify how to guide without fighting. Parents may quote a favorite Bible verse in their answer if they like, including the two verses just read in step 1. Hum a tune and when you stop, identify the holder of the bag. Once all the sentence starters are completed, parents can create their own sentence starter. The sentence starters:

A great alternative to fighting with our teens is talking calmly because . . .

- -

A great alternative to fighting with our teens is being both firm and loving because . . .

- -

Parents who make their kids go ahead and do what they say actually avoid fights because . . .

- -

Physically being near teens—such as walking through or working in the same room when they're doing homework—is a good way to enforce good behavior without fighting because . . .

Deliberately lowering your voice rather than escalating helps you avoid fights because . . .

Giving in is a bad fight-avoidance technique because . . .

Staying firm at first will avoid fights down the road because . . .

Asking who will be there and what they will be doing may bring resistance, but it prevents fights in the long run because . . .

Knowing they can't wiggle out of rules keeps teens from fighting because . . .

Good-naturedly teasing that you are supposed to be mean takes the flame out of fights. A sentence I use to tease well is . . .

Discuss the conversation game with:
- **Which nonfighting tip do you find most powerful?**
- **Too many parents want the youth minister, schoolteacher, spouse, or someone else to do the hard work—to parent or to take the heat—so they excuse that with "I don't want to fight." What's the difference between refusing to fight and refusing to parent?**
- **What parenting pleasures come when you go ahead and calmly but firmly guide your teen to do the right thing?**

3. Attack the Problem, Not Each Other

You'll need a Bible. Post four signs on the four walls: AGREE, DISAGREE, STRONGLY AGREE, STRONGLY DISAGREE.

One way to monitor the effectiveness of your parenting without fighting is to notice that your kids make good choices for their ages and stages. For example, your two-year-old took her laundry to the basket. Your ten-year-old told the truth. Your teenager got his homework done.

In response to groans, sheepish looks, and "my teen doesn't do that" continue:

We all know that getting chores, truth, and homework done requires supervision. These things won't happen unless we're doing our parenting well. So let's find out how to get teens to make the right choices without fighting.

The problem with motivating choices is that conflict feels uncomfortable. We Christians have trouble with trouble. Let's talk about this with a walking discussion. On the four walls are four signs. Move to the one that most closely matches your response to the statement I make. Many of these statements are multifaceted, meaning their truth becomes clearer as we look at them from all four sides.

Gather all parents to the center of the circle of chairs. Remove one chair from four "corners" of the circle so parents can move to the signs on the wall, and read the first statement (*in bold*). Keep in mind the bulleted items as bits of truth you might add as the walking discussion takes place.

Conflict is bad.
- *Differences of opinion can help us all understand something a bit better.*
- *Conflict becomes bad when one person cowers or one person dominates.*
- *Many times parents must be the final authority even when teens disagree, but they can do this without bullying.*
- *Teens may think their parents are mean when they really aren't.*
- *Some parents use their authority to trump a teen's godly viewpoint, and in that case they make conflict bad.*
- *The best solution is to attack the problem rather than each other.*

After all parents have moved, walk to the smallest group to affirm their courage not to follow the mob. Ask someone in that group: **Why do you AGREE (*or DISAGREE or whatever sign that parent stands by*) that conflict is bad?**

Then affirm something about that comment. Even if the statement may not be accurate, you might say:

Many Christians do think that conflict is bad. Perhaps Christians think it is bad because they have seen conflict handled poorly and not the way God would want it handled.

Then move to the next largest group, call on one or two in that group, biblically harmonize their comments, and so on until all four groups have spoken. Call on each parent to speak at least once during the walking discussion, trying to call on everyone equally. Repeat for the other statements.

The major danger in conflict is that both sides think they're right.
- *This is a big danger, but it may not be the major one.*
- *There may be bits of truth on both sides.*
- *Willingness to work things out overcomes defensiveness.*
- *Tone may be even more important than viewpoint.*
- *Stubbornly digging in heels so I can prove I'm right does make "rightness" the major danger.*
- *Parents can hear teens' comments and explain their own in the process of guiding teens through the conflict to the solution.*

If two people disagree, one has to be wrong.
- *If the disagreement is over a matter of morality, one is likely wrong at least to some extent.*
- *Often there are good insights on both sides.*
- *One may be more right than the other.*
- *By pointing out where our teen is right, we parents can overcome much defensiveness.*
- *We could ask teens to point out a tiny place where we're right.*
- *Remembering that teen resistance is not personal or an attack helps parents be level-headed rather than combative.*
- *Even if teens feel we're wrong we must do right (first making certain we are right).*

The main reason fights occur between parents and teens is because the parent won't stand firm.
- *Way too often this is true because teens will wriggle out of a rule when they know they can.*
- *Once kids know their parents mean what they say, teens will cooperate with parents rather than fight their way out of the rule.*
- *Other main reasons fights occur are: (1) parents and teens raise their voices to outtalk each other rather than hear. (2) One wants to win so badly that he or she refuses to work together. (3) People attack each other rather than the problem. (4) Fatigue makes us combative.*

What else makes fights occur between parents and teens?

Time Note

If time is short, do only the first four statements above. Let the following two be supplements if one of the above questions takes less time.

Conflicts can be settled without compromise.

*   *Conflicts can often be settled without changing what is true or what is right simply by discovering what both need and finding a godly solution to those needs.*
*   *Significant compromises such as lying or endangering are not good ways to compromise or to settle conflicts.*
*   *Usually someone has to bend but not always.*
*   *It is NOT healthy for parents to give in to teenagers just to solve the conflict.*
*   *It is also not healthy to impose parental preference just because you're the parent.*
*   *Daily you'll likely have to impose some parental authority such as getting teens to do homework or go to bed.*
*   *Working together is a good compromise.*

Conflicts are best solved by discovering who is right.

*   *Rather than fight each other, fight the problem.*
*   *Notice that there are bits of right on both sides. For example, teens are right in that they do need relaxation in their days, but parents are right that the relaxation comes better after work or homework or chores.*
*   *Who's right is not as important as what's right.*
*   *Doing right is more important than being right or declaring right.*

Invite one or two volunteers to summarize the multifaceted truths they have discovered about how to attack the problem rather than each other.

 Adaptation for a Youth-Parent Meeting

If youth are present, they will especially enjoy the walking discussion. Be certain to openly value their comments to demonstrate to parents how to treasure teenagers without pampering them.

4. Stop Biting

You'll need at least one Bible marker and two cookies for each parent.

Agree that parenting well without fighting is hard but it can be done with God's power. Say: **Let's demonstrate.**

Give each parent a cookie, perhaps a commercially made one, and instruct them to take a small bite out of that cookie each time someone calls out something ugly a parent or teen might say to the other. Start the process by saying:

Call out some ugly words you have heard a parent say to a teenager, and remember to take a bite after each.

Samples:
*   *"You're stupid."*
*   *"You'll never amount to anything."*
*   *"I TOLD you to get your homework done!"*
*   *"My teenager is driving me crazy."*
*   *"I can't wait until my teen is out of the house."*
*   *"It figures that she would act this way."*
*   *"I knew you would mess it up."*
*   *"You can't be a real Christian and do something like that."*
*   *"Why do you do this to me?"*
*   *"I can't trust a word you say."*
*   *"You look terrible—go fix your hair!"*

Write each one on a poster as it is said.

Our culture thinks it's fun and funny to put down teenagers or to complain about them to other parents, but God disagrees.

Call on a previously enlisted volunteer to read Galatians 5:15. Invite parents to tell what happened to the cookies when they bit at them repeatedly. Supplement parent comments with: **Though biting at people has a certain sweetness about it, we will destroy our teens with biting.**

Say: **Well, if we can't say ugly words, what can we say to settle conflict?**

Call for a parent to read Galatians 5:14 ("Love your neighbor as yourself") and wait for adults to explain it.

The way to settle conflict is to lovingly guide rather than bite away.

Write the word *guide* across the poster of ugly words, with a different color marker.

Say: **Our goal as parents is not to win the conflict but to guide our teens toward Christlike behavior. Certainly our teens will buck when we make them treat siblings with kindness, but eventually those two siblings will form a friendship that will weather them through rough times. Coming home will be a joy. Good will result. To guide your teens, use no arguing, no put-downs, just clear expectations followed by loving enforcement.**

Bring out another set of cookies, homemade, warm and fresh from the oven (or at least warmed in the microwave). Then direct each parent to break his or her cookie and share it with the person next to him. Each will then have a full cookie.

When we attack the problem and not each other, we end up with the warmth, closeness, and sweet truth that are demonstrated when we put together two halves of this warm cookie.

Pray for wisdom to guide our teenagers rather than talk about them.

 ## Teaching Tip

> When listing biting and loving comments, ask for "what you have heard a parent say" rather than what "you say"? This gives a little anonymity to the phrases. Then parents don't feel they have to say a "better" bad or a "better" good than another parent. Then in step 5 parents can move toward confession and changing.

5. Love One Another Instead

You'll need at least one Bible and the tree poster(s) from step 1.

Now that we know to guide rather than talk, let's practice ways to do that. Look back at the foundation tree we made at the beginning of the session. Choose one of the foundations and name a "have-to" you will enforce in your home to help that foundation happen.

Circulate to make certain each parent chooses a different have-to and direct them to answer these two questions:

1. How will this "have-to" bring love both in the present and in the future?
2. How can we get this "have-to" to happen with minimal or no fighting?

Samples:
- *For "security in Jesus," a have-to is to attend Bible study and worship every Sunday morning. (1) This will bring love in the present because*

youth will meet other believers with whom to grow friendships. It will bring love in the future because youth will choose a spouse from a churchgoing family which increases the likelihood that the person will be an active Christian. (2) To get this to happen, make it nonnegotiable. If youth don't feel like going to church, get them there anyway just as you get them to school.

- *For "good work ethic," insist that teens get a part-time job and do their chores. (1) This will bring love in the present and future because they will appreciate the work others do for them. (2) To get this to happen, stop providing funds and let teens go nowhere until they land that job.*

6. A Mistake I've Made

You'll need at least one Bible. Stretch a piece of yarn or rope from one side of the room to the other, labeling one side "let go too much" and the other side "control too much."

The tricky part of conflict with teens is that we parents have authority over our teenagers.

It's not an equal partnership like a marriage or a friendship, nor should it be. Some parents err on the side of letting go too much rather than having godly authority. Other parents err on the side of controlling too much rather than having godly authority. There's a line on the floor. I'll call on volunteers to stand where you tend to stay and why. As you tell why you stand where you stand, give a characteristic of godly authority.

Samples:

- *I stand toward the controlling side because godly authority shows what's right and then insists on that right behavior.*
- *I stand a little left of center toward the letting-go side because godly authority helps teens see the reason for the behavior so they can choose right on their own.*

After all parents have stood on the line and added a characteristic of godly authority, gather then in trios to tell one another a mistake they've made in managing conflict with teens and how they believe God wants them to change that.

Adaptation for a Youth-Parent Meeting

If youth are present, change step 6 to talk about goals they believe God wants for managing conflict in their families and two actions through which God wants them to take that step.

7. The Point

Make a copy of "The Point" on bookmark-shaped paper to give to parents.

 The Point

Rather than fuss with each other, take action against the problem. By calmly but firmly showing your teen what to do and why to do it, and then insisting that your teen choose well, there will be less fighting in your home.

"If you keep on biting and devouring each other, watch out or you will be destroyed by each other" (Gal. 5:15).

Once teenagers realize you mean what you say, they will do as you say. As you explain your reasons, they will begin making their own smart choices.

HOME DISCUSSION GUIDE

Send this page home with parents, mailing to any who were not able to attend OR mail to each parent a few days after the session as a follow-up prompter to practice the point.

The Point of our last parent meeting was to stop fussing and start acting. By showing your teen what to do about the problem, fighting will stop.

Showing does not mean to lecture but to link hands and attack the problem. This point is based on the fact that teenagers need parents to show them the way. They fight because they're afraid, because they don't know what to do, or because they think they can wiggle out of the rule. Firm and compassionate action takes the fuel out of the fight and motivates teens to cooperate.

Attacking the problem rather than each other is not a popular solution. More parents complain about their teens than actually parent them. Find motivation to take the narrow road by remembering that guiding well leads to life:

"Enter through the narrow gate. For wide is the gate and broad is the road that leads to destruction, and many enter through it. But small is the gate and narrow the road that leads to life, and only a few find it" (Matt. 7:13–14).

This passage might be paraphrased: "Wide is the gate that leads to fighting and broad is the road that leads to declaring what needs to be done rather than following through. The narrow road consists of equipping your teen to actually solve the problem, and this road leads to life. Your family can be one of the few that finds it."

So together with your teen, pick a problem to solve with the following acrostic. Each of you look at the acrostic and jot down tons of ideas individually. Then blend them into a plan, and work your plan.

The actions to take:

A.*cknowledge there's a problem.* "OK, we both agree that there's a problem. You want me to supply all your money wants, and I want you to budget better. We could define that problem as 'managing money.'"

C.*ollectively list solutions.* "You could use none of my money."

"You could use only my money."

"You could use some of your money and some of mine."

"We could list what you're responsible for and what I'm responsible for."

T.*ogether choose a solution.* "I like your proposal to split the expenses. I need you to be responsible for all your fun money. If you run out, you can find a no-cost way to have fun with friends."

IMPORTANT: Right and wrong are not up for a vote. You as parent can trump any decision. But because your goal is to get your teen to evaluate well and choose well on his own, encourage your teen to contribute the lion's share of the ideas.

I.*mplement the solution.* "Yes, I realize this is homecoming and you want a new dress. But because you've already spent all your fun money, you'll have to wear something you already have. No, you can't have a loan. You must have earned the money and have it in hand before you spend it."

O.*penly say when your teen does well.* "I notice that you drank water instead of Coke at the restaurant. That's a good way to make your money go further."

N.ow move another step forward, not backward. "Yes, you've done well managing your fun money. This year you can take over your clothing budget too. What part-time job would you like to get to finance your clothing?"

During this process this parent guided his teen down the path toward financial independence—no yelling, no fussing; just good, biblical guidance. Managing money well does not come instantly. It takes weeks, months, and years of intentional teaching; but all along the path are signs of encouragement and victory for both the teen and his parent.

What problem will you and your teen attack together?

NEWSLETTER IDEA

Use these as a base for a parent newsletter, for youth-written articles, or for the parent section of the church newsletter.

A Lover Not a Fighter

Sam's dad believes it's not Christian to fight, so he gives in whenever conflict arises. After he gives in, things seem to get worse instead of better. Sam becomes more and more demanding. Sam's dad wonders, *Why aren't things better, when I've done the right thing and avoided conflict?*

Things are worse because there's nothing unchristian about conflict. When a parent avoids conflict, he misses God's solution. Nobody solves the problem. It just sits there and stares back; finally the problem gains enough strength to cause pain. Say Sam wants to go out with friends after the ball game. All the friends are riding in the back of the teacher's pickup truck so no extra drivers are needed. Sam thinks this will be great fun, and if his teacher says it, it must be OK. Sam's dad pictures the whole truckload of kids getting killed if the truck turns over or is hit from behind. Both Sam and his dad are partially right. It will be great fun to go out after the ball game; and riding in the back of a pickup truck is dangerous. Sam and his dad need to harmonize their wisdom to find a solution. But instead Sam's dad lets him push. Eventually he says, "OK, OK, whatever you want to do is fine. I just don't want to fight about it."

Sam learns to push rather than to evaluate the safety of each activity.

Better would have been to say, "Sam, you're right that going out after the game will be fun. You're right that you can usually trust a teacher. But in this case your teacher is forgetting the safety issues. His intentions are good; he's trying to save drivers from having to come. But his solution risks your life and those of your friends. We need to find another solution."

Sam won't thank his dad for taking care of him. Sam will argue. That's a teenager's job, to find out if his dad really means what he says. Sam's dad must change his tune and begin to stand firm:

"But Dad! Everyone else will get to go, and I'll be riding in my parents' car."

"Maybe. But I'll be glad to get together with other parents and offer to drive. Your teacher might even be relieved."

"You can't call my teacher! He'll call me a wimp!"

"I don't have to do that if you can come up with another solution."

"Just let me ride in the back of the truck this once."

"No. That part is nonnegotiable. You'll have to ride in a car with a seat belt. We have to find a solution that includes that detail."

"What if you call a couple other parents and make their kids not be able to ride too?"

"Actually that's not a bad idea. Who would you want me to call? I can't guarantee that they'll forbid it, but I'll keep calling until I find two who will."

"What about Abe and Ben?"

"I'll be glad to start with them."

"And what do I say to my teacher?"

"What about, 'I've decided to ride in a car since my dad's real picky about seat belts.'"

"He may still call me a wimp."

"Or he may call *me* the wimp. Blaming me gets you off the hook. And the 'I've decided' makes you sound powerful."

Through taking action, Sam's dad truly loves his teenager. Turning tail and running only hurts his son.

You and Sam's dad will need God's good power to do all of this, but the peace in your home will be well worth the hassle. Read Ephesians 6:4 and Philippians 4:13 to prod you on.

E-MAIL IDEAS

Choose from these parent support ideas, tips, and strategies especially for electronic transmission. (Remember: Don't create an E-mail Elite; print out and mail the messages to any parents who don't have E-mail).

NOTE to youth worker: Distribute these tidbits of wisdom one at a time, perhaps one a week or one a month.

Guide without fighting, tidbit 1—Fights come from uncertainty, not certainty. So when you give your teen the certainty of consistent rules, your teen will fight less.

Guide without fighting, tidbit 2—It's not you against your teen or your teen against you. It's you and your teen against the evil of the world. So be deliberate about showing your teen what to do and giving her the armor to do well. These "to-dos" include how to study, how to treat family with loving words and actions, how to balance time, and so much more.

Guide without fighting, tidbit 3—Talk over disagreements well by (1) lowering your voice, and (2) raising your expectations of good behavior.

Guide without fighting, tidbit 4—Think of yourself as a gardener: pull weeds of rudeness and selfishness to grow plants of thoughtfulness and loving behavior. Like a good gardener you won't harm the tender plants of goodness as they grow. You'll be just as concerned to nurture the good that's there as you are to pull the weeds that threaten to choke that good.

Guide without fighting, tidbit 5—There's a difference between healthy disagreement and serious conflict. Your teen's viewpoints are important and critical. Hear them clearly to discern what to do about them.

Guide without fighting, tidbit 6—Don't be surprised when your teen bucks. This doesn't mean you're wrong/bad or your teen is wrong/bad. It means your teen wants to know that the rule is strong enough to trust and that you are too.

Guide without fighting, tidbit 7—Tease your teen a bit to take the fuel out of the fight. "Yes, I'm mean. I learned how in mother school." Or, "Well, if I'm unfair, I must be doing my job as a parent."

And if you're sending the E-mail to a cell phone, just use the first sentence of the tidbit.

WHAT TEENAGERS WANT PARENTS TO KNOW

Choose from these questions that invite your teens to share with you anonymous quotes, quips, and comments via E-mail or anonymous survey. Feel free to choose one question at a time as the "Question of the Week."

I'll combine your ideas, with no names or identifying details, to distribute to parents. Feel free to answer a question that's not here or to suggest another question for everyone to answer:

- What do you hate most about fighting with your parents?
- What keeps you from fighting back, as a teenager?
- What have you seen your parents do to keep from fighting with you?
- Tell about a disagreement you and your parents solved (maybe you wanted to go to a place they didn't want you to go to) and how you did it without fighting.

TROUBLESHOOTING

Choose from these tips if your teen keeps on fighting no matter what you do.

Once your family gets into a habit of fighting, it will take time to change that habit. So keep on keeping on. These troubleshooting tips will help:

- Watch your own temper. If you want to win at all cost, your teen will respond the same way.
- Talk honestly about anger but direct it toward the problem. "I gotta admit that I'm really angry about your action, but I still cherish you. So I'm working on being less intense."
- Stress togetherness. "How are we going to change this behavior so you don't make the same mistake again?"
- Monitor. "I know you won't like it, but we're going to keep close touch on this one until the problem is solved. The problem is the problem, but we have to work together to solve it."
- Admit your mistakes. "Yes, I yelled too loud. The reason was worry, but that's not an excuse. Let's take deep breaths and start again."

Bonus Idea

Here is a list of actions for talking through problems without fighting. Display it on the refrigerator and commit to heed these rules. Consider adding one more rule, unique to your family, at the bottom.

This Family Fights Well . . .

1. Because we fight the problem rather than each other.

2. Because we choose to lower our voices when we feel like shouting.

3. Because we close our mouths when we feel like wounding a family member (Gal. 5:15).

4. Because the solution is more important to us than who wins.

5. Because we know feelings will get intense.

6. Because even when things are intense we choose to respond with care.

7. Because we hear all input and then respect parents to guide the process (Eph. 6:1–4).

CHAPTER 3

My Teenager Just Hides in Her Room

So bring her out.

"My teenager never tells me anything. All I ever hear is the slamming of his bedroom door or the dialing of the computer modem."

"Her friends tell me what she's up to; but I long to hear what she thinks, dreams, and feels."

And she longs to tell you. Teenagers yearn to tell the details of their days to someone who is absolutely interested. That's why they spend so much time on the telephone and on-line. They want connections. Teenagers stop talking to parents not because they don't want to tell their parents things, but because something has blocked that communication: time, busyness, disinterest, a previous fight, fear of telling something that may seem silly, or a combination of these. As you deliberately demonstrate genuine interest and make yourself available, your teen will come out of her room to spend time with you. As you hear and help, your teen will talk more frequently and more calmly. As you guide with the same firm compassion that God guides you, your teen will wrestle to the ground the traumas that trouble her.

At first, you may have to force your teen out of her room. This is not pushiness or cruelty. It's a way to keep your teen from suffering in isolation. Your teen may claim to be perfectly fine and perfectly happy, and your teen may actually believe that she is fine. But no one does well when isolated from caring family members. Show you care by regularly connecting and reconnecting with your teen. Otherwise your teen's loneliness will lead to orneriness or risky behaviors. Guide your teen to the delight of family connections.

Goal—This chapter guides parents to engage their teens daily.

PARENT WORKSHOP

Draw from these ideas to lead a one-hour parent workshop.

1. Things to Say

You'll need pencils and paper. Type and duplicate an alphabet response sheet, bringing three for each team expected. Arrange the chairs in two semicircles facing the wall. Divide into more than two teams if you have more than ten parents.

As parents enter, send them to one of two teams according to the first letter of their first names, the first half of the alphabet on one side of the room and the second half on the other side of the room. Challenge parents to write for every letter of the alphabet one question they could ask to get their teen talking to them. Give each team a response sheet with the letters of the alphabet typed vertically down the left side. Suggest they race to fill their sheets first.

Say: **Because many questions begin with W, you can name the topic first, and then the question.**

Samples:
Any news on the friend front?
Been a mostly good or mostly bad day?
Can you tell me more about it?
Definitely that's a good idea. How will you carry it out?
Every day I'm more impressed by your self-control (or fill in another fruit of the Holy Spirit here). What's your secret for expressing that?
Find anyone at school who needed a special touch today?
God poked good into your day how?
How was the test?
I'd love to hear how things went at work.

But What Will We Talk About?

Write for every letter of the alphabet one question you could ask to get your teen talking to you. Race to fill your sheets first. Because many questions begin with W, you can name the topic first, and then the question.

A. _____

B. _____

C. _____

D. _____

E. _____

F. _____

G. _____

H. _____

I. _____

J. _____

K. _____

L. _____

M. _____

N. _____

O. _____

P. _____

Q. _____

R. _____

S. _____

T. _____

U. _____

V. _____

W. _____

X. _____

Y. _____

Z. _____

Joys and sadnesses I can pray about?

Keep me up on how things progress, OK?

Let me know your thoughts and feelings, will you?

Men around you behaving how? Women around you behaving how?

Need some help with your homework?

Open any doors of care today?

Piled-on pressures—what were yours today?

Questions you're wondering about?

Really would love to hear how things are going with your friends.

So, what would you like to do this weekend?

Tell me all about it.

Unbelievable—what happened next?

Valentine's Day can be an abomination. How was it for you today?

Want to take a walk and tell me what happened?

Xplain it to me from your point of view, will you?

You have handled this so well. What's the latest?

Zipped mouth I'm offering. What would you like to tell me that's private?

Applaud the team that finishes its alphabet sheet first.

We raced to write questions that get our teens talking to demonstrate that we have limited times to talk with our teens. It's a race against time to cover everything teens need to know to become independent and happy. In less than six years they will be graduated and living away from our homes.

Then ask teams to alternate calling out questions from their lists, pausing from time to time to affirm or clarify a question. For example, if someone asks an accusatory question, clarify that we use questions to guide teens, not accuse teens.

 **Teaching Tip**

A "trickle-in" activity such as the above one allows parents to engage with one another easily. The listing task gives them something to focus on rather than awkward get-to-know-you moments. It also helps them begin to think about the topic before you introduce it orally. Third, it allows parents to begin to pool their wisdom and see the group as smarter than any one individual. In so doing, they practice the principle of the body of Jesus Christ.

Adaptation for a Youth-Parent Meeting

If youth are present, let them be team captains for this question-listing race. Prepare an alphabet sheet for every teen, and challenge teens to grab parents for their teams as the parents walk in the room. The youth will experience the power of their affirmation, and the parents will experience the joy of being wanted. Ask: **Parents, how did you like being in demand?** *(After many parents have answered, ask:)* **Teens, what did you like about your power to make parents feel wanted?**

Then emphasize that both parents and teens can use their God-given power to encourage and motivate each other toward Christlikeness.

2. Talking Tricks

You'll need these talking tricks duplicated so each parent can have one. Also make a copy of the talking trick paragraphs for parents to teach.

Give each parent a copy of these talking tricks and challenge them to put the vowels back in to find the tricks.

Talking Tricks

The vowels have been removed from these talking strategies. Put them back to read each trick. (HINT: Some are missing more than one vowel; words made of a single vowel such as *a* are left as they were.)

1. CHS QSTNS THT NVT MR THN A YS/N NSWR

2. LNK TLKNG T PRVLGS

3. CNVRS RTHR THN D LL TH TLKNG R LL TH LSTNNG

4. S TLKNG S N NCHR NT A PSTME

5. SHW YUR TN HW T TLK

6. B TH DLT

Call for volunteers to name the unscramblings (*Answers are numbered 1-6 following this paragraph.*) Lightly say that little things like vowels, tone, attitude, and daily communication make huge differences for better or for worse. Then give a copy of each of the following to six parents. Lead in tandem with them as they explain to the group what each one means.

After each, invite parents to then add:

How have you seen this trick work in your household? Remember to say only positive results; no putting down of your teenagers or yourself.

The talking tricks and comments:

1. Choose questions that invite more than a yes/no answer.

- *"How was your day?" invites "Fine." "Did you do OK on the test?" invites "yes" or "no." Instead choose, "What was the best and worst of your day?" or, "Tell me about the test." Use the ABC talking questions we just generated in step 1 to find more samples. Because no teen is comfortable being quiet all the time, and all teens want someone to hear and understand them, no matter how much they claim otherwise, keep on showing your teen how to connect and reconnect. Guiding your teen to talk daily takes time.*

2. Link talking to privileges.

- *"Once you've told me two things about your day, you can get on the phone. But first I need to hear the news."*
- *"If you can't tell me who's chaperoning and a phone number, you'll have to skip the party."*
- *"You can go to your room after you've talked with me about your day."*
- *"If you won't come out of your room to tell me the details of your day, I'll have to take the door off the frame."*

3. Converse rather than do all the talking or all the listening. Teens who talk all the time are selfish because they keep the focus on themselves; teens who never talk isolate themselves and miss the joy of having their ideas heard. Parents who talk all the time lecture rather than genuinely help; parents who never talk come across to their teens as aloof and uncaring. Interaction helps teens learn to hear as well as to express themselves. If you as a parent don't know how to listen and speak caringly, get another parent to teach you. It also helps to treat your teens with the same respect and care you desire from your teen.

4. See talking as an anchor, not a pastime. Talking with your teens is more than passing the time or getting to know each other. It's the vehicle through which you teach your teens how to live life in God's honor. For example, through conversing, you anchor them to truth, to keeping in touch with

Adaptation for a Youth-Parent Meeting

If youth are present, invite them each anonymously to write a *do* and a *don't* for conversation. The *do* is something their own or another parent does to make them feel like talking openly; the *don't* is something that makes them want to clam up. Incorporate these into Step 3 or 4.

4. Tough Talks

You'll need a Bible. Photocopy the following tough times for each team of adults.

Talking well with words and tone are the first steps but not the final step. We must also see the purpose of talking, that every talk is a way to guide our teens toward Christlikeness, either to affirm goodness that is already being expressed or to refine a rough edge. Even a laughing conversation over a good meal affirms the value of family support. Enforcing turn taking during that supper meal refines the look-to-another's-interests-as-well-as-your-own action that imitates Jesus. Let's show and tell each other how to do this.

Give three of these tough times to each team and invite them to dramatize them. Guide teams to assign themselves so each adult has a part in dramatizing at least one solution. For example, two adults might act out the tough time, one as parent and one as youth. A third adult might describe what just happened. Suggest they refer to at least two of the talking tips and one proverb from the Bible as they act out each one with good tone.

 ## Time Note

Give a time limit on preparation and then on presentation for the tough times. Divide your remaining time by six to let you know how much time you have for presentation. Humorously set a timer explaining that you're keeping the wordy groups from going on too long and the shyer groups from too kindly deferring to the wordy groups. Don't identify which group is which. If time is extraordinarily short, cut the preparation time, explaining that many talk situations come up with no preparation.

Tough Time 1—I'd love to try all these talking strategies, but how do I get my teen out of her bedroom? She comes home, grunts at me, and then holes up in her room. If I knock, she says, "Come back later. I'm busy." If I ask her about her day, she says she has to do her homework. When I call her for supper, she says she's not hungry. Then she fixes herself a sandwich after we eat and takes it to her room. How do I get her to talk to us? (HINT: Talking Tricks 2, 4, 6)

Tough Time 2—My teenager is gone so much that we never get to talk. Half the time I don't even know where my teen is. He's home to sleep and leaves our house for school in the morning. But between sports practices, church activities, and going out with friends, he never comes home. I have to ask his friends where he is half the time. (HINT: Talking Tricks 2, 5, 6)

Tough Time 3—I ask my teenager about school, about friends, about interests. But all I get in return are grunts or single-syllable answers. My teen talks to everyone but me. I'm just glad for the youth workers who can get my teen to talk. They keep my teen on the right track. (HINT: Talking Tricks 1, 5, 6)

Tough Time 4—I try to engage my youth in conversation, but my teen says all I do is lecture. I'm trying to tell my teen what he needs to know and how to do things. How can I do this if I don't talk? (HINT: Talking Tricks 1, 3, 5)

Tough Time 5—My problem is that my teenager talks too much. She stays on the phone, on the computer, or holed up with friends. Only occasionally does she have time for me, but even then she does all the talking. I can't get a word in edgewise. (HINT: Talking Tricks 3, 4, 5)

Tough Time 6—I've tried all these strategies; I really have. But my teen still stays quiet. Isn't it possible that some kids are comfortable being quiet? In my family none of us talked. So maybe that's normal. (HINT: Talking Tricks 1, 2, 3)

5. The Point

Make a copy of "The Point" on sheets shaped like a question mark or a T for talk to give to parents.

Thank parents for their extraordinary wisdom. Encourage them to keep sharing communication strategies with one another and to engage their teens in conversation every day.

Give each parent a copy of "The Point" and challenge them to place this point in a clothes drawer or another place where they'll see it as they begin each day.

Invite volunteers to share a single sentence on why it's important to establish and keep daily contact with teenagers. Pray that we heed God's guidance in doing so.

➤ The Point

Establish and keep daily contact with your teenagers. Connect, reconnect, and keep on connecting. In so doing your teen will learn how to talk through both easy and hard times. Through honest and caring sharing, teach your teen to live these proverbs, while you exemplify them yourself:

The tongue that brings healing is a tree of life,
But a deceitful tongue crushes the spirit (Prov. 15:15:4)

The words of a man's mouth are deep waters,
But the fountain of wisdom is a bubbling brook (Prov. 18:4)

A man of knowledge uses words with restraint,
and a man of understanding is even-tempered (Prov. 17:27).

Teens want to tell the details of their days to someone who cares. As you demonstrate genuine interest, your teen will talk more and more calmly.

HOME DISCUSSION GUIDE

Send this page home with parents, mail it to any who were not able to attend, or mail to each parent a few days after the session as a follow-up prompter to practice the point.

The Point of our last parent meeting was to establish and keep daily contact with your teenager.

This point is based on the way God woos, pursues, and stays in contact with us. When parents stay involved with teens' lives, teens find the power to do the right thing for the right reason. Teens discover that life is something we do in God's glory and something we do as a team. "What good is it, my brothers, if a man claims to have faith but has no deeds?" (James 2:14).

Together with your teens establish some house rules for talking. Sit down at the kitchen table with a paper tablecloth and all write ideas on it at once. *Samples:*

- *Each of us will share something about our day, every day, with all the others.*
- *Each of us will show interest in what the other says rather than make fun of what the other says or thinks.*
- *I'll take the chip off my shoulder. You'll take the chip off your shoulder.*
- *Rather than assume the other is attacking us, we'll take constructive criticism constructively and assume the other wants to help.*
- *We'll choose carefully our tones and words so the other doesn't feel attacked or belittled.*
- *We'll take turns, none of us monopolizing the conversation or refusing to speak.*
- *We'll point out each other's strengths as well as help each other's weaknesses.*

After you've filled the tablecloth with ideas, let each family member tell about the ones they named. Listen with rapt attention to each other.

Direct each family member to pick one or two favorites. Arrange them so they spell an easy-to-remember word. Our sample list could spell:

Attacks nonexistent; instead we help each other (was 4 and 7).
Refuse to monopolize or give the silent treatment (was 6).
Remove chips and defensiveness (was 3).

Everyday interchange (was 1).

Show interest (was 2).

Tones and words chosen lovingly (was 5).

Consider letting your teen make a refrigerator poster of the talking rules.

NEWSLETTER IDEA

Use these as a base for a parent newsletter, for youth-written articles, or for the parent section of the church newsletter.

"But I'm Not Doing Anything Wrong!"

All your teenager does is hide in her room. What's so wrong about that?

The problem is not being in her room; it's isolation. When your teen avoids interacting with you, she misses the love, support, and instruction a parent is uniquely qualified to give. Many teens love their rooms. A little private time there is no big deal; everyone needs a bit of solitude. But when teens harbor in their rooms or claim you can't come in, there's a problem. The basic problem is not drugs or alcohol or secluded conversations with seedy friends—although those may be present. The root problem is loneliness. Teens need connections with family to keep them rooted, happy, and growing. If your teen is doing wrong things in her room, address those directly and immediately. But even when there are no outward problems, make connections.

Here are some sample room remedies, moving from simple to severe. The simpler solutions prevent problems. The more severe ones solve problems:

- Spend some time in your teenager's room, sitting on the bed and talking. When you come willingly into your teen's domain, your teen may more willingly come into yours.
- Knock before entering, but walk on in almost immediately. Knowing you can walk in at any time keeps your teen from the temptation of doing something wrong.
- Converse every day. When you show regular interest in your teenager, your teen will want to tell you what's going on and will want to be near you.
- Put no television in teen rooms. Television has a tendency to isolate and confuse unless two or more people deliberately watch it together

and talk about what they see. So have only one television, the one your family watches together in a family room.

- Allow no friends of the opposite sex in your teen's bedroom except for "Wanna-see-my-room?" tours. You come along even on those.
- Take the telephone out of your teen's room. Buy a cordless phone instead so that you know when your teen is on the phone and for how long. This is not a punishment but a communication that your teen does not have to go off alone to talk to people. There are people in your house to talk to as well. Cordless phones also allow you to keep the phone from taking over homework time. Explain these reasons to your teen.
- Insist that the door stay open, and keep your bedroom door open except for occasional moments of privacy. Let doors be closed for minutes rather than hours.
- Remind your teen that his or her room is a privilege, not a right.
- Refuse to allow your teen to declare his or her room off-limits to you in the name of "privacy." Your option to look through things is not an invasion of privacy but a protection against temptation. Explain that you will not exercise this right just to be nosy.
- Take the door off if your teen refuses to keep the door open.

E-MAIL IDEAS

Choose from these parent support ideas, tips, and strategies especially for electronic transmission. (Remember: Don't create an E-mail Elite; print out and mail the messages to any parents who don't have E-mail).

One of the best ways to engage your teenagers is through E-mail. Many teens are more comfortable with on-line communication than with face-to-face communication. So use E-mail and on-line chats as a bridge to other forms of communication, and then keep using it as a communication approach that's good in itself.

IMPORTANT: Let E-mail be positive communication only. Save the tough talks for face-to-face talks so each of you can see the other's reactions as well as words. Some ideas:

Sunday—Send a note affirming something about the way your teen honored God at church, such as: "I saw the way you scooted down to make room for Pat. That was loving like Jesus loves."

Monday—Send a sentence prayer about the new week, such as: "Just want you to know I'm praying for you at school this week, especially for that one friend situation and the test that's coming."

Tuesday—Send a Bible verse to encourage your teen, such as: "And my God will meet all your needs according to his glorious riches in Christ Jesus" (Phil. 4:19).

Wednesday—Ask a question to get your teen thinking about how to live for God, such as: "What do you think is the best action that shows you love others as you love yourself?"

Thursday—Thank your teen for something she or he taught you about God, such as: "I watched you talk that problem through calmly and give your brother a new start. Thanks for prompting me to do the same."

Friday—Bless a plan your teen has made. "I'm glad you will be spending the night with Terry. You've chosen a great friend."

Saturday—Invite your teen to work on something with you, such as, "What do you think is the next project we should do on the car?"

Note to youth worker: You may want to divide this message into one for each day and send it on that day.

And if you're sending the E-mail to a cell phone, send the day and idea without the sample.

WHAT TEENAGERS WANT PARENTS TO KNOW

Choose from these questions that invite your teens to share with you anonymous quotes, quips, and comments via E-mail or anonymous survey. Feel free to choose one question at a time as the "Question of the Week."

I'll combine your ideas with no names or identifying details to distribute to parents. Feel free to answer a question that's not here, or to suggest another question for everyone to answer:

- What is something fun your family has done together?
- What are some things you enjoy doing with each of your parents?
- What are some questions your parents ask to get you talking about what you think, dream, and feel?
- Why do teenagers still like spending time with their parents?
- What makes teenagers hide in their rooms?
- What has one of your parents done to coax you to communicate with them, and why are you glad your parent did that?

TROUBLESHOOTING

Choose from these if a teen does not display the expected behavior.

Suppose you've been trying to talk with your teen and your teen stays quiet. What should you do?

- Go places together. Your teen will be finished processing things by the time he gets home. But if you're in the car together, he'll talk on the way home. Go together even if your teen is of driving age.
- Take a walk together. Exercise absorbs nervousness, so it becomes easier to talk.
- Work on a chore together such as doing dishes, dusting, or cleaning out the garage.
- Volunteer to drive your preteen's group. Kids talk in the car like you're invisible.
- Implement a talk-and-then-you-can-_____ rule. "After you tell me two sentences each about two events from today, you can get on the computer."

Bonus Idea

Follow this checklist to pray through your engaging actions.

Possible way to use: Give each parent three copies. Suggest they use one a week, keeping one as the master to reproduce as they run out. They may want to change the filled-in checkpoints to meet a current situation in their family.

Let God Check You

☐ 1. God, on a scale of one to ten, how well am I being the adult—deliberately guiding my teenager to communicate well and refusing to pout or feel sorry for myself?

☐ 2. God, on a scale of one to ten, how well do I talk with my teen, rather than talk about my teen or talk at my teen?

☐ 3. God, on a scale of one to ten, and because each is critical to full love from a parent, how well do I balance affirmation with instruction?

☐ 4. God, on a scale of one to ten, how well am I teaching my teen to communicate thoughts and ideas?

☐ 5. God, on a scale of one to ten, how well am I teaching my teen to communicate feelings and needs?

☐ 6. God, on a scale of one to ten, how well am I teaching my teen to welcome others' thoughts and ideas, feelings and needs?

☐ 7. God, on a scale of one to ten, how well do we keep communicating even through rough or emotional times?

☐ 8. God, on a scale of one to ten, how well am I _____?

☐ 9. God, what word describes how well I engaged my teen this week? _____

☐ 10. God, what do you want me to repeat, delete, or change next week? _____

CHAPTER 4

My Teen Doesn't Want to Be Seen with Me in Public

So show your teen how to be independent.

"My teen walks ten paces in front of me and acts horrified if I speak to him in public. Are all the good times over?"

"I still want to go places and have fun as a family. I don't remember growing another head. Why is he suddenly so embarrassed to be seen with me?"

Because he wants to be seen. Your teenager wants to be known as himself, not as an extension of you. He wants people to see him as a capable and likable person, rather than the son or daughter of a capable and likable person. So your teen's refusing to walk with you actually has little to do with you and everything to do with his becoming an independent person.

He's also more than just a wee bit worried that you'll do something that onlookers will interpret as weird. If he's standing next to you, they may reject him too.

Does that mean you stop walking with your teenager? Not necessarily.

Sometimes it means you follow him secret-service style, close in the background but not hand-in-hand. Most times it means you walk next to him but behave extraordinarily well.

You are working yourself out of a job, but relax. You aren't working your way out of a relationship. You and your teen can, and should, stay close all of your days. It's just a new kind of closeness with a greater level of maturity.

Goal—This chapter guides parents to show their teens how to manage each new step of independence. Parents work their way out of a job by teaching each new level of responsibility.

PARENT WORKSHOP

Draw from these ideas to lead a one-hour parent workshop.

1. What I Like about My Teen

You'll need for each adult five individually wrapped fruit-flavored chews such as Starbursts and a bag of individual chocolate candies such as M&Ms or Reese's Pieces. Bring a chalkboard or poster. Set up a circle of six chairs for a variety of sports such as baseball, soccer, basketball, football, tennis, and more. Label each circle with a sign that says, "We like watching or playing (name of sport) best."

As parents enter, give each five different fruit-flavored chews and warn them not to eat the candies until you tell them how to do so. Gather parents in teams of about six based on their favorite sport to watch or play. Set up a circle for baseball, soccer, basketball, football, tennis, or other sports, choosing the number of sports by the number of parents you expect. If one (or more) team stays small, combine teams, moving the sign with the team. Direct the members of each team to tell the team five things they like about each of their teenagers, tossing a piece of their candy in the middle of the circle for each compliment they give their teens. When all group members are empty-handed, instruct them to hold up their hands.

Say: **Sometimes we fear that the teen years are the end of all the sweetness with our offspring. We fear we'll be empty-handed, that we won't get to share any more times together, any more laughs, any more goodness. But these fears don't have to come true. Our teens may not want to walk with us at school ball games, but they will walk with us in other places. They may go out with their friends more, but home is always their best place. They will be able to do more and more on their own, but they will continue to need our love and steady guidance. The teen years are the start of a new kind of sweetness.**

Invite adults to call out popcorn style a sweetness they have shared with their teenagers recently.

Samples:
- *A good long talk in the car*
- *A laugh over supper*

- *Remember-when-I . . . ?*
- *Storytelling with grandparents*

Toss parents a chocolate candy such as an M&M for each sweet time they name, but caution them not to eat them yet.

After all have shared, coach all to eat the candies.

Say: **Notice the mark this candy left in your hand. Notice also the sweetness of the moment it hit your tongue. Parenting teenagers as they grow toward independence is similar. We must look for, cherish, and continue to generate sweet moments rather than whine about small messes.**

Pause to pray that we will listen to God's guidance as we parent through the years of independence.

Say: **There's another way these candies represent parenting teenagers toward independence. Each of the chocolate candies you just ate was a different color on the outside, but each tasted the same on the inside. Teens worry that people won't see them the way they are inside, that people will judge them by outer appearances or may lump them into one big group. They fear that their dreams won't be seen and their thoughts will be dismissed. They long to be known, and loved, for who they are, not as an extension of their parents and not as a generic teenager. These are some reasons they don't want to be seen with us parents in public. It's also the reason they worry so much about appearances.**

In reality, each teenager is unique, like the different-tasting fruit chews in the middle of your circles.

Prompt parents to recall good qualities about their particular teenagers. Invite parents to name a way to cherish their own teenagers as unique and worthy-to-be-known individuals.

Samples:
- *Hear their dreams.*
- *Show them steps toward achieving their dreams.*
- *Call them by name.*
- *Spend time with them individually and regularly.*
- *Teach them skills so they will be competent and not just feel competent.*
- *Remember yesterday's concern and ask about it today.*
- *Overcome stereotypes such as "all youth like to talk on the phone" and "all guys like sports" because not all kids do. Instead get to know each teen.*

- *Point out where they're smart.*
- *Ask: How can I help you?*
- *Give and equip to manage responsibility.*
- *Repeat what they said to show you understand it.*

As each parent shares, let them pick and eat one of the five fruit chews, which are now mixed into one big pile.

Write on the chalkboard: "Give your teen opportunities to become more and more competent."

Say: **During this session we're going to focus on the competence issue, to parent our unique teens in ways that keep them actually sweet. Only as we show our teens how to handle the responsibilities of independence can they stay sweetly likeable.**

Call on a parent to read Deuteronomy 6:4–7.

- **When are we supposed to teach our teens how to love our Lord with all our heart, soul, and strength?**
- **How have you specifically done this, or could you specifically do this?**

Pray once again that we will listen to God as He shows us what's inside our teen and how to unwrap our unique teens to love our God through sweet independence. **We'll eat the other four fruit chews as the session goes on, so leave the rest in the middle of your team's circle.**

2. How My Teen Gets to Know Others

You'll need the four fruit chews per parent left from the previous step and the chalkboard or poster. Enlist three parents to do the skit and make a copy for each. Make three name tags: "Parent," "Teen," "Friend."

The first step toward healthy independence is to give your teen opportunities to become competent. This can be as simple as being quiet when someone comes up to talk to your teen.

Write on the poster: "Through letting them practice." Call on three parents you have already enlisted to present this skit. The friend can be an adult youth sponsor or a peer. Overexaggeration is perfectly fine.

Teen and parent walk along talking. A friend approaches from the other side of the room. The friend approaches and speaks directly to the teenager. This friend can be a peer or an adult youth worker.

FRIEND: "Hi, how was your weekend?"

PARENT: *(Enthusiastically interrupting the teen to answer for him/her)* Oh, thanks for asking. It was great. B.J. went to the Christian concert and then to the youth party afterward. Oh, it was the BEST concert B.J. was telling me.

FRIEND: Um, cool. Well, B.J., do you want to come by later? A bunch of kids from school are coming.

PARENT: *(B.J. starts to answer, but the parent again interrupts.)* Oh, you are so nice to ask! I'm sure B.J. will want to be there, won't you, honey?

TEEN: *(nods)*

FRIEND: *(hesitatingly)* OK, good. B.J., come on over between 6 and 6:30.

(Friend walks the other direction.)

TEEN: Mom! *(or Dad depending on who plays the parent)* Why did you do that? Don't you realize I can talk for myself?

PARENT: Of course, I do, honey. You don't have to get so uppity about it. Be respectful!

TEEN: Oh, you just don't understand!

What happened here?

Pause for parents to interpret the situation. Then continue with these questions:

Whose need was the parent meeting?

Samples:

- *Parent thinks he was meeting the teen's need but actually was meeting the parent's need to talk.*
- *Parent may have been trying to be friendly to the friend.*
- *Parent may have subtly feared the teen wouldn't talk.*

What could have happened if the parent had just been quiet for a few seconds longer?

Samples:

- *Teen could have spoken for self.*
- *Teen could have competently carried on a conversation.*
- *Teen could have realized his/her ability to speak independently.*
- *Friend and teen could have connected independently.*
- *Friend could grow respect for the teen.*

Why is it hard for us parents to be quiet and let our teens talk and do other tasks of life for themselves?

Samples:

- *We're naturally talkative.*
- *We fear we'll be rude if we don't speak.*
- *We simply aren't thinking.*
- *We may be trying to help the friend feel comfortable.*
- *We like the friend too.*

How do you or can you or any parent in the skit keep quiet in public?

Samples:

- *Count to ten or twenty.*
- *Wait however long it takes for the teen to speak.*
- *Smile at the friend rather than speak so parent won't feel snobbish.*
- *Parent reminds self what good company my teen is.*
- *Decide to share the limelight with my teen rather than hoard it even accidentally.*

What equally bad thing could happen if the parent was too uninvolved?

- *Teen would learn from friends rather than parent.*
- *Parent wouldn't be there to affirm teen's good choices and refine teen's dangerous choices.*
- *Teen would miss parent's guidance.*
- *Teen could pick bad friends.*

What other strategies have you used to let your teens establish and maintain their own relationships without totally abandoning them?

Samples:

- *Hang out after church rather than rush your teen home to give your teen time to interact with other teens and adults.*
- *Arrange time to spend with grandparents.*
- *Have parties at your house.*
- *Thank adults who invest in your teen.*

What sweet results have occurred when you were quiet and let your teenager talk?

Samples:

- *I get to watch someone enjoying my teenager.*

- *I get to watch my teenager engage someone in conversation.*
- *I get to see my teen as a person rather than an extension of me.*

Adaptation for a Youth-Parent Meeting

If youth are present, guide them to present a set of rules they would like their parents to obey such as: (1) Don't wear embarrassing clothing. (2) Be calm rather than silly in public places. (3) Walk three steps behind me if a cute someone approaches. Challenge the youth to present these rules in humorous ways, perhaps including consequences for parents not following the rules such as, miss your Sunday nap.

3. How to Equip My Teen for Independence

You'll need a fine-point permanent marker, the three remaining fruit chews per adult, the chalkboard or poster from step 2, and circles of tape. Change the chairs to one large circle with the fruit chews in the middle. It's OK to mix them up.

Carrying on conversations is one of many skills independent adults need. But giving your teen opportunities to get to know people independently won't help at all if your teen is no fun to know. You have to teach your teen character traits of independence that others will enjoy.

Write on the poster: "Through intentionally developing characteristics of godly independence."

What are some characteristics of godly and competent independence?

Direct the one with the birthday closest to today to name a good character trait. Then call for each adult around the circle to name one, none naming what another names. As they name a trait, write it on the wrapper of a fruit chew and give it to them, but instruct them not to open it.

Samples:
- *Honesty*
- *Responsibility*
- *Genuine interest in others*
- *Good humor*
- *Wise money management*
- *Interest in people*
- *Drive/motivation*
- *Good guy-girl skills*
- *Security*
- *Sensitivity*

- *Thoughtfulness*
- *Respect*
- *Lack of self-centeredness*
- *Good conversation skills*

Guide each parent to name a way to unwrap the character trait written on the fruit chew wrapper, and then to eat that candy. Gather the wrappers as they are unwrapped and tape them to the poster with tape circles you made before class.

Samples:

- *Honesty—opened by modeling the truth and giving stiff penalties for any kind of lie.*
- *Responsibility—opened by showing teens how to establish habits that get work, chores, communication, and homework done with less pain and more sense of accomplishment.*
- *Genuine interest in people—opened by noticing when your teen shows interest and affirming it.*
- *Good sense of humor—opened by telling jokes that always make the hearer feel loved.*
- *Good money management—opened by letting teens take over more and more of their expenses and refusing to bail them out. Examples: Fun money by eighth grade; gas money by tenth grade; all clothing by twelfth grade.*
- *Drive/motivation—opened by finding something your teen loves to do and getting the supplies/lessons that will help your teen grow the skills to exercise that passion.*
- *Security—opened by having house rules: No one puts another down whether family member or guest.*
- *Sensitivity—opened by showing your teen how to help someone in pain, such as taking a meal together to someone grieving or baby-sitting for a mom whose other child is in the hospital.*
- *Thoughtfulness—opened by coaching siblings to talk out disagreements and enforcing rules like not slamming siblings.*
- *Respect—opened by treating every person as though he's the last person on earth.*
- *Other-centeredness rather than self-centeredness—opened by giving tasks that make that teen critical to the operation of the family.*

How does showing our teens how to be independent bring sweetness to their lives? To yours?

 Adaptation for a Youth-Parent Meeting

If youth are present, begin step 3 by inviting them and their parents to name qualities they like in other people. Then direct them to name ways they would like their parents to help them develop these same qualities.

4. A Specific Plan That Could Work with My Teen

You'll need Bibles, the two remaining fruit chews per adult, masking tape, and the poster from steps 2 and 3.

Gather parents back in their original teams and direct them:

Choose one of the independent skills and develop a detailed plan for what you could do to develop it in your teen.

Write on the poster: "Through making a plan and working your plan." Overview this sample first and then guide parents to make their plans:

To manage money:

1. Take your teen to the bank to open a checking account.
2. Watch while the banker shows your teen how to keep the checkbook.
3. For a while supervise each check written and entered.
4. Guide your teen to get a part-time job if he doesn't already have one.
5. Show him how to save a percentage, give a percentage to church, and spend a percentage.
6. Show him how to deposit the savings regularly and only spend after the savings and church percentages are allocated.
7. Show him how to stop spending when you run out, and to not spend what you don't have by refusing to lend money. Romans 12:12 fits here because our teens can wait and creatively budget as parents do when money is short.
8. Refuse to bail out your teen so he learns to manage better the next month. Otherwise he'll learn that no matter how much he overspends, he can always get more money. Talking and pleading won't help. Only letting him take responsibility will do it.

Suggest parents look in such passages as Romans 12 for ideas as they make their plans. Provide paper, extra Bibles, and pens. As each plan is presented, discuss with questions like:

Is there another step any of you would add to this plan?

Tape each plan to the wall.

5. The Steps We'll Take Toward Independence

You'll need the last fruit chew. Cut a piece of poster board into six stair steps—three large steps will make two pieces that stack to produce six steps; place them leading up to the poster for steps 2-4. Label each step 7, 8, 9, 10, 11, and 12. Prepare a small set of six steps for each parent to take home.

Independence is not an instant bestowal but a set of steps. It's good to provide one new responsibility coupled with a privilege each year.

Write on the poster: "Through giving a new responsibility each year."

During approximately what years of your teen's life would you place each of the plans we have just developed?

Let each team choose its span, and write it on the stair-step poster you have created, one step for each of the six years from seventh to twelfth grades. Each team will have added a step to each year, so there will be many options.

After each team has its plan on the master steps, pass out a small replica of the stair-step poster to each parent, created by cutting six steps from an 8½-by-11-inch sheet of paper. Direct each parent privately to write the six plans they will implement with their own teenagers, talking to God as they make their selections.

Say: **Inviting God to guide your choices, choose a step of independence for each teenage year. Of course, steps will carry over into subsequent years, and you'll do preparation in previous years, but your teenagers will like looking forward to the privileges of each year.**

Samples in addition to the plans made by teams:
* *Seventh—Get to sit with the youth group in church.*
* *Eighth—Manage clothing budget with set amount provided by parents.*
* *Ninth—Attend guy/girl party.*
* *Tenth—Get to drive one person in car and perhaps go on dates.*
* *Eleventh—Get a job and take over part of own expenses.*
* *Twelfth—Lead family group made of younger teenagers at church.*

Pray that God will guide each parent to produce happily responsible teenagers.

 Time Note

If time is almost over, skip step 6.

6. A Walking Plan

You'll need Bibles and paper Xs.

End on a lighter note: how to walk with a teen in public.

Turning teens loose in the mall or a theme park is not safe or wise, especially if your family is going together to those places. But walking next to one another may not allow others to get to know your teen. So you can walk in proximity with one another, similar to the way secret-service agents protect and follow a dignitary. Or you can back off and be busy when an adult or teen approaches to talk with your teenager. Or you can sit at the back of the movie theater while your young teens are in the front. Or you can try other approaches.

Give each team of adults three paper Xs about two inches high and direct them to place and move the Xs to demonstrate at least three game plans for walking with your teen in public, similar to the way a ball coach would draw a game plan diagram.

Call for each team to present at least one of its game plans.

How does positioning yourself to give your teen attention bring sweetness to both you and your teen? How might you use the same principle in teaching other independence skills?

The Point

Make a copy of "The Point" on colorful paper shaped like an arrow to give to parents.

Give "The Point" to parents and explain:

This point is put in an arrow to remind you that your actions will point your teens toward successful independence. Without equipping your teens, they can't make it on their own. Coach well!

➤ The Point

Give your teens increasing responsibilities and show them how to manage those responsibilities.

"These commandments. . . . Impress them on your children. Talk about them when you sit at home and when you walk along the road, when you lie down and when you get up" (Deut. 6:6–7).

Nobody's born knowing how to do independence well. Your teen is depending on you to show them how to be a responsible and likable person. In this way your teen can be truly independent: to do the right thing for the right reason as an expression of love for God.

 Teaching Tip

Duplicating "The Point" takes a lot of time. Can't parents pick their own main point? Yes they can, but all of us remember better what we see, hear, and touch. Sending home "The Point" reinforces what parents learned. They can, of course, add other things they learned, but this main one challenges them to act and shows them how.

HOME DISCUSSION GUIDE

Send this page home with parents, mailing to any who were not able to attend or mail to each parent a few days after the session as a follow-up prompter to practice the point.

The Point of our last parent meeting was to give our teens increasing responsibilities and show them how to manage those responsibilities.

Teens can't be happily independent if they can't manage their lives. When they manage their money, relationships, and time well, they find and give happiness. God pictures this process as a daily sharing of wisdom and strategies: *"Impress them on your children. Talk about them when you sit at home and when you walk along the road, when you lie down and when you get up"* (Deut. 6:7).

Nobody's born knowing how to do independence well. Your teens are depending on you to show them how to be responsible and likable people.

In this way your teens can be truly independent—to do the right thing for the right reason as expressions of love for God.

Give your teens and yourself a copy of this word block. Challenge each other to find the thirteen ways to be independent. This can be done by putting a line between each word:

EARNANDMANAGEMYOWNMONEY
CHOOSEWHATTODOWHENPICKAFASCINATING
CAREERANDWORKHARDEVENIFMYJOBISNOT
PERFECTBUILDMYOWNFRIENDSHIPCHOOSEASPOUSE
ANDGROWAGOODMARRIAGEDECIDEWHAT
LIFESTYLEGODWANTSMETOLIVEBEHONESTWITHOUT
ANYONECHECKINGUPONMEUSEHUMORTOBUILD
PEOPLEUPRATHERTHANBELITTLETHEMMOTIVATE
MYSELFTOGETTHEHARDSTUFFOFLIFEDONEBUILD
EMOTIONALPHYSICALANDSPIRITUALSECURITY
RESPONDTOHUMANNEEDINTHEWAYJESUSWOULD
TAKECAREOFOTHERSNEEDSASWELLASMYOWNNEEDS
DOALLTHISASMOTIVATEDBYLOVEFORGOD

Then take turns picking one of these questions to answer:
1. To which independence skills do you most look forward?
2. Which independence skill do you already do well, and how did you learn it? (Parents, be certain to affirm teens by answering this.)
3. What independence skill worries you?
4. What would earn independence privileges?
    Samples for choosing what to do when:
    • Freedom to stay up as late as I want is earned by getting up fresh and on time each day.
    • Freedom to go to the mall is coupled with choosing someone else to walk with.
    • Freedom to go camping is coupled with choosing a parent to camp in the next campsite.

NEWSLETTER IDEA

Use these as a base for a parent newsletter, for youth-written articles, or for the parent section of the church newsletter.

How to Be a Nonembarrassing Parent

Lower your voice. What you consider a normal voice sounds like a megaphone to your self-conscious teen. If you whisper or talk so low that only your teen can hear, your teen will feel less like the whole world is listening in.

Enjoy your teenager. During the avalanche of worrying what people think, provide a warm outcropping that your teen can hide under. In this safe place your teen knows without a doubt that one person absolutely likes him—you.

Be secure. Certainly adults are adolescents who are just a little older. Put aside your needs for attention and recognition long enough to be totally content in who God made you to be. Why? Your teen will draw on your strength.

Demonstrate. Your teen needs to watch how a steady someone behaves in public. You're able to greet people with grace, to refuse to be manipulated, and to guide situations so they produce togetherness. You worry less about how you look and more about how you treat people.

Follow the Rules. Don't holler out "Love you!" as you drop your teenager off at school. Wait until your teen is in the car and the windows are rolled up before you start to talk. Step back three paces when a friend approaches. Let your teen pick the table in the restaurant. Invite your teen to make rules for speaking to him or her in public. You'll, of course, undergird these by refusing to do anything unwise or immoral.

Tease. A little humor goes a long way to lighten the weightiness of the path toward independent identity. Always tease in ways that make your teenager feel treasured instead of trashed, encouraged instead of belittled.

E-MAIL IDEAS

Choose from these parent support ideas, tips, and strategies especially for electronic transmission. (Remember: Don't create an E-mail Elite; print out and mail the messages to any parents who don't have E-mail).

To prod powerful independence, your teen needs sailing skills. You must check the weather and your boat before setting out. In most weather, things go smoothly as long as you follow established procedures. In some weather, you batten down the hatches and add extra manpower. In other weather, you never venture out because you and your boat will get crushed. Similarly there are places teens should never go even when seventeen, eighteen, or nineteen. There are places some sixteen- to eighteen-year-olds are ready for that thirteen- to fourteen-year-olds are not. And all places need the instruction of parents in basic skills such as conversation, honor, politeness, and security.

Equipment you must impart to your teen through modeling, training, and enforcement includes:

- Honesty—Faking it or lying have no place in true maturity.
- Work—Giving your best to what needs doing is the basis for competence. Doing your best also honors God.
- Taking responsibility—If you spend all your money, wait until you earn more to spend more.
- Time management—Everyone can choose to get both work and play done in the time you have.
- People skills—Getting along, solving problems, and sharing the good and bad of life are critical.
- Sensitivity—Look not only to your needs but to the interests of others (Phil. 2:4).

Give the privileges of independence only when it is learned and earned through the above actions. You'll have to show the skill, practice them with your teen, and then let her take charge.

Note to youth minister: You may want to divide this message into "The Independence anchor for this day is . . ." and add one of the anchors.

And if you're sending the E-mail to a cell phone, here's a short one: Independence isn't doing whatever you want whenever you want. It means being smart enough to choose the smart path on your own.

WHAT TEENAGERS WANT PARENTS TO KNOW

Choose from these questions that invite your teens to share with you anonymous quotes, quips, and comments via E-mail or anonymous survey. Feel free to choose one question at a time as the "Question of the Week."

I'll combine your ideas with no names or identifying details to distribute to parents. Feel free to answer a question that's not here or to suggest another question for everyone to answer:

- How do your parents spend time with you in public without totally embarrassing you?

- What are some places you and your parents go publicly together in town?
- What out-of-town places do you go, and what do you like to do there?
- How would you explain to a parent why you do not always want to walk right next to a parent?
- What do friends' parents do in public that you wish your parents would do?

TROUBLESHOOTING

Suggest these actions to implement when a teen does not display the expected behavior.

Parenting toward independence seldom happens like solving a clean algebra problem. It's more like simmering a good soup. It takes steady actions over a long period of time. Here are tips to help your parents keep on keeping on:

- Get together with other parents to establish the same rules. For example, no one goes to the mall alone or to nightclubs. We parents will take turns chaperoning camping trips.
- Write a letter telling your teen the independence skills you see him or her express. This will give the motivation to keep on taking on responsibility.
- Continue the learning, earning, and maturing process. (See Home Discussion Guide above.) Just like in school, different teenagers need different teaching approaches, but *all* teenagers need parents who will persist in teaching them until they learn.

Bonus Idea

This idea is a set of strategies for independence.

Possible way to use: Print and fold as a worksheet you can mail to parents. Encourage them to fill in the last four sections based on what they chose in step 5 of the Parent Workshop.

Sample Paths Toward Independence

Independence doesn't happen simply because a teen hits a certain birthday.

Independence happens as parents teach their teens to actually act responsibly.

All teens need persistent training that matches privileges with responsibilities.

1. Teach a teen to manage money by opening a checking account with the teen's own funds, showing her how to work the checkbook, and letting her pay her own fines and earn her own from interest. Let your teen fund all free time money and later all clothing from her own funds.

2. Teach your teen to be responsible with a car by letting him pay for his own gas and insurance, as well as any tickets or insurance increases. Offer free gas for responsible behavior. Let him use the family car rather than a car of his own.

3. Teach pride in a job well done by praising liberally when your teen works hard at any household task. Assign a specific household tasks that your teen manages regularly.

4. Teach responsible relationships by insisting that your teens speak civilly to family members and friends. Pull computer privileges or other freedoms for ugly talk.

5. Teach responsible learning by insisting that homework be done before any free-time activity.

6. Teach responsible service by serving together in a church or community project.

Teach all the above and more by doing these well yourself and letting your teen see you do them.

CHAPTER 5

My Teenager Thinks I'm Made of Money

So demonstrate how work brings freedom.

"Every time I turn around my teen is asking for more money."

"No matter how much I explain the value of a dollar, my teen just spends like the supply is unlimited."

The key to good money management is experience, not talk. Your teen will not appreciate what you're giving her if you just give better and give longer. Your teen must manage money for herself, reaping both the benefits of good management and the penalties of poor management. Only as your teen administers her own money will she learn the value of a dollar. Only as she must supply her own money will she discover ways to make each hard-earned paycheck stretch as far as possible.

In addition to spending money well, teens must avoid the dangers of assuming things will make people happy. They must skirt the traps of buying on credit and taking resources for granted. Money is a "big ten" issue because it is tied to three of the Ten Commandments. Both you and your teen have likely struggled with at least one of these three commandments:

"You shall not covet your neighbor's house . . . wife . . . or anything that belongs to your neighbor" (Ex. 20:17).

"You shall not steal" (Ex. 20:15).

"You shall have no other gods before me" (Ex. 20:3).

Money is also a contentment issue because both parents and teens must learn to be content whether well fed or hungry, whether living in plenty or in want (Phil. 4:11–12). They must learn to balance money-earning with church involvement, school, and other life commitments. Money is the root of all kinds of evil, and misusing it brings great grief no matter how unintentional that misuse was (1 Tim. 6:10).

Finally, money is an issue of stewardship. Teens and parents reap happiness when they choose to use money and other resources to the maximum (Phil 4:13).

When our children were tiny, it was our responsibility to take care of all their needs. But as they grow, our responsibility becomes working ourselves out of that job by giving them the joy of providing responsibly for themselves.

Goal—This chapter guides parents to equip their teen for managing money. Parents will voice why teaching responsibility shows deeper love than serving as a money hand-out service.

PARENT WORKSHOP

Draw from these ideas to lead a one-hour parent workshop.

1. More Than a Game

You'll need construction paper, markers, masking tape, and for each team a stack of three-by-five-inch cards and a strip of masking tape. Tear for each circle a strip of tape about six feet long and tape it, sticky side up, in the middle of each circle of chairs. Do this by turning under the ends. Write and get ready to post a poster with this statement: "The parents' job is to gradually but definitely hand over all financial responsibility to our teenagers."

As parents enter, gather them in teams according to the age of their teenagers. If your group is small, create a team for parents of middle schoolers and a team for parents of high schoolers. If your group is larger, create one team for each grade or two. Challenge each team:

In the center of your circle is a stack of cards. Write on each card something for which your teens want or need money. Then lay these end to end, the short sides on the tape so each card takes up three inches of tape. The trick is that each money-spending thing must begin with the letter the previous one ended with. You are racing to create a longer strip of money-spending than any other team.

As more parents come in, direct them to the team that matches them. Walk to each group and continue to motivate, giving more tape as they fill the strip they have.

Samples with which to prompt ideas:
- *Clothes*
- *Spending money*
- *YMCA dues for exercising at YMCA*
- *A fee for the church mission trip*
- *Pizza*
- *Additional parts for stereo*
- *Overdue fees at library*
- *You need gas in the car*
- *Ring for girlfriend*
- *Date funds*
- *Senior ring*
- *Gotta have senior pictures*
- *Stuff for college*
- *Extra food for when friends come over*
- *Reading material like magazine subscriptions and books*
- *Some eating-out dollars*
- *Shoes*
- *Some great jeans*
- *Set of wheels to get around in*
- *Notebook paper for school*
- *Lots of tickets for ball games, plays, and more*

Call time and prompt teams to tape their idea strips to the wall, one under the other. Applaud generously the longest strip.

Teenagers want and need to buy a lot of stuff. We listed these things in strips to demonstrate that spending money on one thing tends to lead to spending money on the next thing. We parents can feel overwhelmed at the financial demands of our teenagers. What are some of the questions we parents must ask to decide what to do about all these things that cost money?

As parents call out questions, write each on a piece of construction paper, and tape them to the wall. Or give each parent a sheet of construction paper and let the parents write the questions and display them. Supplement with these questions:

1. What should I buy, and what should my teen buy?
2. What must be purchased now, and what can wait?
3. What quality of each item should I buy?
4. When are brand names worth buying?
5. How do I get my teen to earn and spend money well?
6. What principles of financial management do God and I want my teen to practice?
7. What is a need, and what is a want?
8. When are wants worth buying?
9. Where can we save money?

Say: **We'll address several of these questions during this session. But first know this critical truth: Our job in finances is gradually but definitely to hand over all financial responsibility to our teenagers.**

Pause to pray that God will help us teach our teens financial responsibility so they can honor God with their resources.

Ask: **Why is helping our teens develop financial responsibility more loving than serving as a money hand-out service?**

Wait for several parents to respond.

How does giving our teenagers fewer material things help them grow content? Why must we practice the fewer-things principle also?

 ## Adaptation for a Youth-Parent Meeting

If youth are present let them join each team. They may also want to hang the posters as groups complete them.

2. Minitalks on How to Build

You'll need a Bible, the wall of questions from step 1, a set of building blocks, a stack of paper, and a marker that writes on clear tape. Tape a piece of clear tape on the side of each building block.

Guide all parents to pull their team's chairs together into one large circle.

Perhaps the first question is to find out what God wants our teenagers to understand about money. What do they need to know? What actions do they need to practice?

Write on the side of a building block that has been taped with clear tape to protect it: "Gradually but definitely hand over financial responsibilities" and place it in the middle of your circle.

This is one foundational principle of teaching our teens good and godly financial management. What others would you name?

Give each parent a block on which you have attached clear tape. Make available markers that write on clear tape. Guide parents to take turns writing a principle of money management on their blocks, with or without a Bible verse reference. Call for each to name the principle and add the block to the tower. Provide paper so adults can draw a copy of the tower as it is being built. Suggest they might want to take it home to remember the ideas of this brilliant group of parents.

Sample money management principles and ways to use them:

- *Balance money-earning work with church sense (Eccl. 3:1).*
- *If you don't have the money; don't spend it. Borrowing money is seldom a good idea (Rom. 13:8).*
- *Save a percentage, put a percentage in church, and spend the rest as God would spend it.*
- *Buy essentials first. We must pay for school supplies before buying a stereo.*
- *Balance work hours with church, school, and family time (Heb. 10:24–25).*
- *Always find a way to save a little here or there. Examples: Buy a subscription rather than individual magazines. Get a smaller package of senior pictures. Buy a car that's a year or two old rather than a brand new one.*
- *Buy generic brands rather than name brands when quality is not an issue. If your teen wants the name brand, he or she pays the difference.*
- *Try to find at least some things on your list that you can do without. Don't buy them.*
- *Find God's way to take care of needs (Phil. 4:19).*
- *Be sure money or big ticket items don't own you (1 Tim. 6:10).*
- *If you don't have money to buy something you need or want, wait until you earn money to buy it. In the meantime find a creative way to do without. For example, if you have no money to go to the movies and dinner, meet your friends after the movie and ask them to tell you all about it while you drink water at the restaurant. Or rent a video.*

Once all the blocks are in place, call on one or more parents to read aloud Philippians 4:11–13 from their Bibles, preferably in at least two translations. The NIV translation reads: "I have learned to be content whatever the circumstances. I know what it is to be in need, and I know what it is to have plenty. I have learned the secret of being content in any and every situation, whether well fed or hungry, whether living in plenty or in want. I can do everything through him who gives me strength."

What principles of financial management do you see specifically in these verses? How do you see the principles in our block structure living out those principles?

Encourage several parents to give ideas.

Samples:

- *Not spending before you have the money helps you be content when you are in need because the times of need will be fewer (you won't have interest payments).*
- *Earning your own money makes sure you are fed, clothed, and sheltered.*
- *Buying a subscription helps you be content when you are in need because a magazine would come when you have no money and you could enjoy a good read.*
- *Buying generic brands would make times of plenty last longer because there will be plenty tomorrow as well as today.*
- *Saving a percentage, giving a percentage to church, and spending the rest as God would spend it helps you be content when you have plenty.*
- *Finding a way to save a little money with every purchase helps you manage your finances with God's help.*
- *Buying essentials first helps you manage your finances with God's help.*

Lay down a paper that says "YOUTH" and ask:

How would you transfer one of these principles to your teenagers?

Call for each parent to choose a block different from the one he or she named and to move it to a second pile to represent transferring it to teenagers while they explain how they would actually transfer it. Example: *I would transfer "if you don't have money to buy something you need or want" by letting my teen see me not rushing out to buy more after the month's grocery money is gone. Instead we'd make a feast out of what's in the house.*

If the blocks fall down, pick them up and build them again.

Say: **Sometimes things fall down as we teach. We simply pick up where we were and start again.**

Move to another wall these and similar questions written during step 1 to indicate that you have addressed them during this step:

- What principles of financial management do God and I want my teen to practice?
- What is a need, and what is a want?
- When are wants worth buying?
- Where can we save money?

Use parents' comments.

Say: **Money management is more than a side issue. It becomes a main issue if we don't learn it early.**

Also many youth ministers and parents hate part-time jobs because they pull youth away from church. The problem is not the job, but the lack of balance. Some youth work so much that they have no time for church or school. They are paying for cars and other big-ticket items. Other youth have no job, convinced that others should fund their mission trips and church supplies.

Just as all Christians must learn to balance jobs with family, and money-earning with money-spending, teens must learn to balance work with church involvement, and money-earning with money-spending. When teens get part-time jobs, they have the potential to become even better youth group members. Why? Because they learn time management, balancing of life, stewardship, teamwork, commitment, and many more Christlike qualities.

Balance is the key. So help your teens live Romans 12:1–2 at its best, whether physically at work, in the church building, at school, or at home. As a youth worker I plan to. Send them notes to ask about their jobs. Mail Bible study outlines or handouts to any who can't be there. Together we can communicate that your youth are salt and light in their schools, at their jobs, and when at church.

Call on a parent to reread 1 Timothy 6:10 to show what can happen if we don't manage money well.

 **Time Note**

Most groups have one or two members who talk so freely that they will unwittingly monopolize the group. Humorously using a timer helps equalize talking without putting these parents on the spot. Set your watch for sixty seconds, or set another kind of timer. You can also limit responses to one sentence, not allowing any to talk a second time until at least three others have spoken. Why is it important for all parents to talk? Because the one who talks is the one who will learn.

3. Practice Makes Perfect?

You'll need a Bible, and a photocopy of the three strategies. Place several 1s, 2s, and 3s in an envelope and let parents choose one without looking to be assigned to their teams.

To hand over financial responsibilities and learn how to balance work with church, school, and home, our teens must have money to manage. Let's debate which of three strategies could be best for teenagers to learn financial responsibility.

Divide adults into three teams by drawing a number from an envelope you have prepared. The 1s are on one team, the 2s on another, and the 3s on a third. Challenge them to argue that their plan is the best for teaching good financial management, adding biblical principles as they can.

1. *Strategy 1*—Let a teen manage one of the budgets we fund for them. For example, middle schoolers could manage a set amount of clothing budget. They could do this by semester with half of the money allotted in July for the months through December and the other half allotted in January for the months through June. If they spend all their clothing money in February, there will be no money for a swimsuit. They could do without, go to a yard sale, or otherwise solve their situation of "want."

- -

2. *Strategy 2*—Let teens use their own money earned from a job for specific areas. Do not allow big purchases such as a car until teens have covered smaller responsibilities. Help by showing how to take savings, tithe, and set expenses off the top. Help them know how many set

expenses to take on; for example, if they have a mission trip payment, they won't want to put a new coat on the check card. You'll help your teen manage savings accounts and balance the checkbook. Then you'll help him manage a credit card, insisting he pay it off every month.

----

3. *Strategy 3*—Your teen comes to you with each purchase she needs and you grant or deny it, explaining the reason for each yes or no. In this way you model the principles of evaluating purchases, saving here and there, and deciding what to buy when. For example, if you want to teach saving in little ways to add up to big ways, take your teen with you when you shop for groceries. You save a penny or two on each item, and it becomes huge at check-out time. You'll also want to let your teen listen in on some of your money discussions.

Guide the debate according to principles of informal debates, except adapt it for a three-way debate. Example:

1. Each strategy team has three to five minutes to prepare its presentation, including assigning points to each team member.

2. Each strategy team speaks for ninety seconds on the strengths of its strategy.

3. Each strategy rebuts the other two for thirty seconds each.

4. Each strategy has a closing minute to speak, rebutting the rebuttals.

Circulate while teams work to remind them that each parent must speak during the debate, and each must speak for the same amount of time, perhaps six parents taking fifteen seconds of its presentation, and ten seconds of each rebuttal.

Say: **Our informal debate was designed to bring out the strengths of each of the three responsibility-teaching strategies. Part of their strength is determined by when you use them and how you use them.**

Discuss with questions like:

1. If you used all three in your home, in what order would you do them and why?

2. Which one is better for younger youth and why? For older youth?

3. How do the circumstances determine which one you'll use?

   Example:

   • *If my teen spends too much or too little, I might use 3.*

- *If my teen wants to spend freely and without worry about what comes next, I might need to use 2.*
- *If I have been using 1 or 3, it might be time to take the next step of 2.*

 **Teaching Tip**

If all three of these money-management strategies have strengths and weaknesses, why not just say that? Why bother debating? Because through debate parents must find those strengths and weaknesses to make their points. Wrestling with a point of view is one of the best ways to understand that viewpoint, including both nuances and obvious elements. So don't spill the beans by saying all three have strengths and weaknesses; let parents discover that themselves and tell you what those strengths and weaknesses are.

4. Who Pays for What?

You'll need the strips of ideas from step 1.

All this theory does little good if we don't actually apply it. In the debate you have identified several good application actions that would teach your teens financial management. Another action is to separate what you need to buy and what your teen needs to buy. Let's practice this.

Direct each team to take apart its step 1 strip of money requests by tearing the tape between cards, and then to separate the cards into two stacks, one stack of items the teen buys and one stack the parents purchase.

While teams work, move to another wall these and similar questions written during step 1 to indicate that you will address them during this step:

- What should I buy, and what should my teen buy?
- What must be purchased now, and what can wait?
- How do I get my teen to earn and spend money well?

Call for each team to report its findings. Invite reasons for why they sorted as they did. Then ask teams to shuffle once again and separate the list between what the parent buys and what the teen buys if the teen is a college freshman. Again report findings.

What plan of action might get you from your teen's present spending habits to where you want your teen to be as a college freshman?

Samples:
- *Give a little more responsibility each year.*

- *Keep on insisting on church involvement even when working.*
- *Don't bail out once you've said your teen is responsible for a certain aspect of spending.*
- *Explain that people are more cautious when they spend their own money.*
- *Let your teens see you involved in church even though you work.*

What difference does it make that the teen is younger or older? What stays the same?

Samples:
- *Younger teens take on less financial responsibilities but still cannot spend more than they have.*
- *Younger teens don't have car or gas expenses but still must find ways to save.*
- *Younger teens can't earn as much so they must spend within their means.*
- *A small responsibility for a seventh grader is as important as a large responsibility for an eleventh grader.*

What difference does it make that the teen has or does not have money?

Samples:
- *A teen cannot use the excuse of not having money to spend parents' money.*
- *If a teen does not have money, you can still teach financial management tools like waiting until you have money or earning money to get what you want.*
- *Letting your teen not have money is a good motivation to go ahead and get a job.*
- *You can let teens watch you spending while they wait to get old enough to earn money.*

What if you have a teenager who begs and pleads for money, making you feel bad for not giving it to him or her?

Samples:
- *Your feeling good or bad doesn't determine right or wrong.*
- *Financial responsibility determines what's right or wrong.*
- *Hold firm because your teen needs the security of knowing that begging is not the way to get money.*

Our job in finances is gradually but definitely to hand over all financial responsibility to our teenagers.

Sort a third round, this time sorting into six piles—the expenses a teen should take on during each grade, seven through twelve:

Seventh—spending money for movies and going out to eat, plus any overdue fees at the library

Eighth—gifts for friends

Ninth—all of the above plus half of all church trips

Tenth—all of the above plus gasoline money (do *not* give a car to teenagers; let them earn one in college or later)

Eleventh—all of the above plus music and part of senior ring

Twelfth—all of the above plus all clothes, and supplies for college (graduation money comes in handy here!)

What if the teen has no money, earns no money, or runs out of money?

After several comments, blend them to explain that the solution is clear.

Just like you and me, if they don't have money, they don't spend money. They don't go to the movie, on the church trip, or to the other event. They don't get a class ring or that new pair of jeans. They don't spend until they earn, no matter how they beg.

5. Job Jabber

You'll need a Bible, large sheets of paper, and markers.

For youth to take over more and more financial responsibilities they must have a job. Your teens may not want a job or may say they can't find one. Don't argue about this. Simply stop supplying money.

Invite parents to tell how they have done this and how it works for their teenagers. Agree that it's hard not to give in to our teen's pleadings, but only as our teens begin to provide for themselves can they experience the joy of good money management and of balancing work with church and home. Supplement as needed from the Home Discussion Guide and Newsletter Article.

Then guide parents to return to the teams they were a part of when they first arrived. Provide large paper and markers to each team and challenge them:

Write on your paper at least ten jobs a teen could get in your community. Include different jobs with the same company. For example, a teen who works in a restaurant could bus tables, greet, or work the cash register.

Sample jobs and categories:
- *Babysit*
- *Mow lawns*
- *Fast food*
- *Grocery stores*
- *Factory work*
- *Filing and phone answering*
- *Retail*

Allow 126 seconds for this assignment, humorously calling out times such as 99 seconds, 38 seconds, and so on.

Call for a count of the jobs each team created and add them for a grand total. Applaud. Then invite teams to take turns calling out their jobs.

Pray that our teens will find just the place God wants them to serve through a job this year.

Then guide another round. Give another large sheet of paper, a marker and 126 seconds.

Say: **This time name all the ways youth could serve God in a part-time job.** *Samples:*
- *Cheer up customers.*
- *Never cuss.*
- *Always say encouraging words to coworkers.*
- *Give an honest hour's work for an honest hour's pay.*
- *Refuse to steal from bosses by giving away food to friends.*
- *Treat every customer as though he were Jesus.*

Play a third round. Say: **This time name strategies for staying involved at church and keeping grades up while working.** *Samples:*
- *Get to church at least once each week.*
- *Care for someone in Jesus' name.*
- *Do homework before work when possible.*
- *Keep hours under fifteen hours a week.*
- *Serve weekly at church.*
- *Find a way to serve God at work.*
- *Request no Sunday hours, or to be off Wednesdays.*
- *Refuse big ticket items, such as cars, to keep work hours reasonable.*

Pause to thank God for the ability to serve Him through our jobs.

6. Here's What I'd Do

You'll need a Bible and the lists/principles displayed on the wall from steps 1–5. Reproduce the case studies so each parent can have one.

As time allows, let parents choose one of these case studies. **Demonstrate what you would say and do to model how work and good money management are the most freeing path for each of these teenagers. Use at least two ideas from the lists and principles we have generated through this session.**

Pete goes from job to job, not staying at any job more than two weeks. One time the boss was too mean. Another time his supervisor wouldn't let him off for an event Pete wanted to attend. Still another time Pete was late, and the boss fired him. Pete says he needs to borrow money.

- -

Rachael says she's too busy to work. She has church activities, mission trip preparation, peer tutoring at school, homework, exercise, home chores, and more. Since she's doing so many good things with her time, she wonders why you won't just support her. After all, you have plenty of money.

- -

J.B. wants the best. Only brand-name clothes will do. Waiting for sales isn't an option. Because J.B. wants it, you've always felt it important to provide it. But you're getting into trouble financially because of over-spending so regularly. J.B. wonders why you won't buy things like you used to. Don't you care?

Adaptation for a Youth-Parent Meeting

If youth are present, invite each one to give a sixty-second testimony about how they have chosen to honor God through the way they act at their part-time jobs. If some do not have part-time jobs, prompt them to talk about how they honor God through house/yard chores or other manual labor. Let youth know about this assignment ahead of time so they can think through what to say.

HINT: Even if they've never consciously honored God before at work, they will start now because they have thought it through.

The Point

Make a copy of "The Point" on green to give to parents.

➤ **The Point**

Give your teen increasing accountability to earn and manage his or her own money and to balance money-earning with the rest of life.

"I have learned to be content whatever the circumstances. I know what it is to be in need, and I know what it is to have plenty. I have learned the secret of being content in any and every situation, whether well fed or hungry, whether living in plenty or in want" (Phil. 4:11–12).

When teens discover that God will equip them to manage both money and all issues related to it, they find true freedom. They manage every penny as though it is God's and in so doing they find pride in a dollar well managed.

As parents depart, encourage them to think about the nonmaterial riches they give their teens when they insist on honorable work and happy responsibility.

HOME DISCUSSION GUIDE

Send this page home with parents, mailing to any who were not able to attend, or mail to each parent a few days after the session as a follow-up prompter to practice the point.

The Point of our last parent meeting was to give your teen increasing accountability to earn and manage his or her own money.

This point is based on the fact that God will help us manage our money and resources whether times are good or bad.

"I have learned to be content whatever the circumstances. I know what it is to be in need, and I know what it is to have plenty. I have learned the secret of being content in any and every situation, whether well fed or hungry, whether living in plenty or in want" (Phil. 4:11–12).

When teens discover that God will equip them to manage both money and all issues related to it, they find true freedom. They manage every penny as though it is God's, and in so doing they find pride in a dollar well managed, and in a life well spent.

Demonstrate this by pulling out your Scrabble® game or another game with letter tiles. Play according to the game rules, except keep ten or more letter tiles at a time.

Challenge your family: "Rather than words, we must spell phrases that show the nonmaterial riches that come when we work honorably and take responsibility for our financial and other resources."

Riches your family might spell include:
- Happypride
- Peopleskill
- Enough
- Sharing
- Giving
- Doitmyself
- Maturity
- Independence

Play another round and name blessings we can bring through working. Samples include:
- Attention
- Findproduct
- Giveidea
- Profits
- Stayinbusiness
- TreatlikeGod

Play another round of money traps to avoid. Samples include:
- Too many hours
- Buying on time
- Dropping out of school
- Dropping church
- Letting money own me
- Cars and expensive stuff

Finally play a fourth round and name jobs through which a teen might bless others. Samples:
- Fastfood
- Greeter
- Waitress

- Bagger
- Clerk
- Cashregister
- Bookstore
- Grocerystore
- Construction
- Hardwarestore
- File
- Type
- Janitor
- Orderfiller

Thank your teen for playing this game with you. Explain that both the way we play and the way we work can honor or dishonor God. Then thank your teen for playing this game with a good and caring attitude and working with a godly spirit. Even if your teen never has before, your interest will motivate a great work ethic. Then let your teen see you demonstrate the same good work ethic.

NEWSLETTER IDEA

Use these as a base for a parent newsletter, for youth-written articles, or for the parent section of the church newsletter.

Riches Worth More Than Money

So your teen won't get a job.

You know all the theory. You know the value of pride in a job done to God's glory (Col. 3:23). You've talked until you're blue in the face. But you haven't been able to get your teen to land a job.

Begin by recognizing that few people would work if they didn't have to. Your teenager is not selfish as much as she is unexposed to the world of work and the good that comes from doing a good job in honor of God. You'll have to force the job-finding process; but with the right job, your teenager will triumph and will develop a great work ethic. She'll become a better church member, a better student, and a more caring family member.

Just as with so many aspects of parenting, all you need is a little action. Adapt this series of conversations for your wonderfully unique teenager:

"Rachel, you must find a job by next Friday," you explain.

"But Dad, I've tried!" Rachel responds.

"Yes, I know you have. You likely need to dig into sources you haven't yet tried. Sit down with me here a minute, and we'll lay out a plan." You get out paper and pen, and Rachel rolls her eyes.

"Dad, I *really* have to get my homework done."

"I understand. This will only take a moment."

You keep your word by rapidly listing these steps:

1. Pick up at least six applications.

2. Take the applications back within twenty-four hours. I'll help you fill them out.

3. Call back for interviews within forty-eight hours.

4. Pick up more applications if those interviews don't pan out.

5. Let me know when you begin.

"And what if I do all that, and I still don't have a job?" said Rachel.

"Well, I know you'll get something because the fast-food restaurant is hiring as is the grocery. You can work there if none of your other choices work out."

"Dad, I already explained that I'm not going to work with food. Fast-food is too greasy, and grocery work is too boring."

"Then find something else, or do that until you get another job. Most of us have to pay our dues at our second or third choice before landing the job we really want."

"Working with food isn't even on my list."

"You may have to add it. You must have a job by next Friday, or you lose car privileges and phone privileges."

"That is totally unfair!"

"Actually, it's more than fair. The car and phone cost money, and I've been funding them for you for a long time."

"But Dad, you have a full-time job and lots of money. I have to go to school and want to serve through church."

"I want to serve too. And your getting a job is more than just earning money. It's pride in a job well done for Jesus; it's learning to work with a team; it's being independent. It's learning to find the 'time for everything' that God teaches in Ecclesiastes."

"But Daddy, I'm glad to be dependent on you," Rachel says with her charming brown eyes that turn you to mush.

"And because I love you so much, I want you to have the joy of independence. I want you to make your own godly money choices. You're a good person, and I want people to see your skill," you say just before she wraps you totally around her finger.

No matter how skillful your talk, you'll now have to follow with action. You'll actually have to take away car and phone privileges, even if it means driving her everywhere yourself and monitoring the phone until she lands a job. You may have to physically take her to job interviews. You'll have to follow through to make certain she actually gets (and keeps) that job.

It's not all hard. Sooner than you realize, you'll be hearing stories like, "Fast-food is still gross, but I got to make this one customer really happy today. I think God liked that. And my boss let me off on Sunday!"

E-MAIL IDEAS

Choose from these parent support ideas, tips, and strategies especially for electronic transmission. (Remember: Don't create an E-mail Elite; print out and mail the messages to any parents who don't have E-mail).

Send one of these Bible promises for money management to your parents of teens each day, or each week:

"The love of money is a root of all kinds of evil" (1 Tim. 6:10). So don't assume that giving your child money is a way to show love.

"Godliness with contentment is great gain" (1 Tim. 6:6). So notice nonmaterial things that bring contentment to your teen and compliment your teen each time your teen finds contentment.

What if your teen has too few funds to stretch over many expenses? She can call on God's help because "I can do everything through him who gives me strength" (Phil. 4:13). Your teen may have to sell a car, stop a service, or refuse a purchase so the money will stretch.

Working well is a way to honor God, as explained in Romans 12:1: "Offer your bodies as living sacrifices, holy and pleasing to God—this is your spiritual act of worship." Invite your teen's ideas for honoring God through work as you share your strategies with your teen.

And if you're sending the E-mail to a cell phone, here's a short one: Today spend each penny in just the way Jesus would spend it.

WHAT TEENAGERS WANT PARENTS TO KNOW

Choose from these questions that invite your teens to share with you anonymous quotes, quips, and comments via E-mail or anonymous survey. Feel free to choose one question at a time as the "Question of the Week."

I'll combine your ideas with no names or identifying details to distribute to parents. Feel free to answer a question that's not here or to suggest another question for everyone to answer:

- What do you like and not like about being responsible for making your own money?
- What financial responsibilities should be yours? Your parents? *(Example: Who should buy the car and gasoline, and why?)*
- What is the secret to balancing work, church involvement, and school?
- Do you think teenagers as a whole are mostly responsible or mostly irresponsible with money? What would make them more responsible?
- How can you tell that you are working too much or too little? How can you adjust expenses?
- How have your parents helped you learn how to manage money?
- What does contentment have to do with money management?
- What is the secret to keeping money and work from taking over your life?
- What else do you wish your parents would do to help you manage money?

TROUBLESHOOTING

Suggest these actions to implement when a teen does not display the expected behavior.

Suppose you've tried to get your teen to get a job, and your teen won't do it or keeps losing a job.

- Give a deadline after which your teen goes nowhere until a job is landed. At that point begin withdrawing privileges of mobility and contact. Also physically go with your teen to be certain your teen gets a job.

- Give no money for any reason—drive your teen to school and church, write checks for necessities such as school fees, and put away your available cash. The need to spend will motivate your teen to earn.
- Tie work to a privilege your teen wants such as using a cell phone.
- Affirm your teen for jobs well done.
- Teach and model job skills such as honoring God at work, balancing work, school, and church, and doing your very best wherever you are.

Bonus Idea

This idea is a guide to making work fun.

Possible way to use: Enlarge, print, and mail to all your youth parents. Suggest they keep one side for themselves and give one side to their teen, as an expression of partnership in honoring God.

Making Work Fun

Colossians 3:23: *"Whatever you do, work at it with all your heart as working for the Lord, not for men."*

See your work as a challenge, as a way to honor God, as a way to fund church and daily expenses, and as a ticket to independence.

Example: "Even though I look like a mere grocery sacker, I am actually a small-child cheer-giver. I do this by listening to children's stories and telling them where they are smart."

To honor God at work:

1. Look for someone to cheer up.

2. Look for a person to relieve by doing your job well.

3. Look for a need to meet such as safety, food, competence, attention, and more.

4. Look for a kind word to say about a coworker's efforts, as a way to love like Jesus loves.

5. Do the job in honor of those you care about—your mom, yourself, your dad, your God.

CHAPTER 6

My Teenager Doesn't Like Himself

So like him boldly until he can act with competence and confidence.

"I love my teenager. I see her gifts, her wit, the delight she displays. But she just can't see it."

"I tell my teenager that I like him all the time. But he still won't pick up his room or finish his homework."

Liking self involves both confidence and competence. You can't just tell your teen he's wonderful, though you must do that. You must show him how to be wonderful, how to use the skills he needs to live well and love well. And you must show your teen how to do this selflessly. It really is true that you must die to self to be happy. It really is true that you must lose your life to find it. If you don't show your teen how to give selflessly, how to persist through trouble, and how to do without something from time to time, your teen will become a *prima donna* convinced that you and everyone else owes him happiness. He will stay miserable and make everyone around him miserable.

How do you do this? Through daily loving. Expressed love at home is the most powerful way to give teens a foundation for emotional and intellectual security. But that love must be both words and actions. Telling your teenager that he's brilliant will do no good if you don't also make certain that he gets his homework done and understands how to take a test. Without doing homework he can't keep up in class or learn the material. Without taking tests well, he can't demonstrate what he's learned. Brilliance comes through actual learning, not just talking about it. Without action your words are simply meaningless ways to give your teen the big head.

Goal—This chapter guides parents to bless their teenagers deliberately, regularly with both words and training.

PARENT WORKSHOP

Draw from these ideas to lead a one-hour parent workshop.

1. What Blessings Look Like

You'll need a square of foil or a lump of modeling clay for each parent. Arrange the chairs in one big circle.

As parents enter, give each a square of foil or lump of clay, and direct them to shape a model of one person blessing another while sitting in the large circle of chairs you have arranged for them. If you have more than ten parents, arrange circles of about eight chairs each.

Parents may look quizzically at you when you give this assignment.

Say: **One human giving a blessing to another is an abstract concept— one that's hard to put into words—so let's make a picture of it.**

- **How do you know a blessing when you see one?**
- **What's a blessing you've received?**
- **What's a blessing you've given?**
- **What shape might a blessing be?**
- **How might you bless your teen in a way God has blessed you?**

Walk around and encourage parents, actually blessing their efforts by noticing wise sculptures, assuring parents they can sculpt what a biblical blessing is, hearing parents' questions, and even preapproving sculptures if parents want that. The blessings parents shape might be symbolic, object lessons, pictures of actual blessings, ways to bless, even words.

Samples:
- *"Two interlocking rings are a symbol of a blessing because a blessing links people to God and to each other."*
- *"This foil is shaped like a blanket because when my dad blessed me, I felt all warm and secure."*
- *"My mom used to wave to me every morning as she said, 'Have a God-filled day.' So I shaped a waving hand."*

- *"I bless my husband by listening intently and asking questions that show I care about the details. Then he blesses me by doing the same. So I shaped a question mark."*
- *"I shaped the word YOU because most blessings are personally designed, like 'I'll think of you all day today.'"*
- *"God blesses me by giving me resources to solve whatever comes. So I shaped a purse to represent a treasure trove of resources."*

Give a one-minute warning and then call for all parents to present their sculptures. Give a sentence of affirmation about each sculpture, explaining how that sculpture helps the group understand an aspect of blessing.

After all blessings have been presented, explain:

Say: **Unless you make a living at sculpting, you may have felt a little uneasy shaping foil (or clay). Teenagers feel similarly uncomfortable about some of the tasks of adulthood they must undertake. But I deliberately blessed you by walking around and giving you words of encouragement, with the goal of helping you complete your task. Your wisdom and ideas were there the whole time; the blessing just drew it out. You can do the same thing for your teenager by blessing your teen deliberately and regularly. During this session we'll explore how to do this.** After adults add comments continue by saing . . .

Express real love every day in your home. This love is not just mushy words but also cooperative living. Each day mention reasons living with family is rich and fun. Each day follow through with your teen treating other family members well and other family members treating your teen well. Share chores. Encourage one another through problems and pressures. Celebrate selflessly with the other. Persist through tough times rather than try to make them instantly OK. Then living with your teen will genuinely be fun. And your teen will see evidence of this everywhere she goes.

Why bother? Confident teenagers live their faith in God more boldly. Secure teenagers are less prone to temptation and wrong choices. Persist-through-trouble teenagers pick good friends and later a good spouse. The key to this confidence is competent actions expressed by skilled teens in real life. Every teen has gifts worth growing, and every teen can make others happy. Courageously love your teen so he will know and express this.

💡 Teaching Tip

Why not just explain the impact of blessings rather than put parents through the discomfort of sculpting? Two reasons: (1) First, if parents actually experience the discomfort of a new and unfamiliar task and then the joy of mastering it, they can grasp a bit of the anguish their teens experience at managing the new and unfamiliar tasks of adult life. (2) Sculpting guides parents to go deeper and wider into the meaning of blessings. It's easy to repeat what they've heard said about blessings. But parents must actually understand blessings to sculpt one.

2. What Blessings Contain

You'll need for each parent a Bible, a pen, and a triangle of paper. Cut triangles by folding a corner of an 8½-by-11-inch sheet to the other side, cutting off the strip, and then cutting apart the two right triangles. Write a sentence strip with this section of Hebrews 10:25: "But let us encourage one another." You will add a bit of the verse to the wall for every step until the whole verse is up there.

Say: **Blessings tend not to happen unless we become deliberate about giving them.**

Review several facets of blessings that parents brought out in their step 1 sculptures, one from each parent if possible.

A good blessing must have these three aspects:

1. **It must be true. If it's not true, it betrays God's command not to bear false witness, not to lie. Also teens can see right through a fake.**
2. **It must include genuinely loving words. Teens want to hear us say we love them and believe in them. They need to hear it over and over to believe it (and hearing includes not just speaking but sending E-mail, writing letters, and more).**
3. **It must be demonstrated through equipping actions. Our words become empty if no actions back them up. For example, we may tell our teens they are brilliant but then not make them complete their homework. They can't be brilliant if they aren't learning at school. The ability to learn is there, but it must be expressed to become a true blessing.**

As you teach the three aspects, pause between each so parents can write that aspect on one of the three sides of a paper triangle that you give them. At the end each side will have one of the three aspects. Provide pens for those who need them. Then guide them to copy from their Bibles Hebrews 10:24–25 in the center of the triangle.

Guide parents to practice the "encourage one another" phrase from Hebrews 10:24–25.

Say: **Now we'll practice blessing one another as this verse recommends.**

Call for each adult to name how the sculpture created by the parent to his or her left helped him or her better to understand *blessing*. Smile and affirm each blessing as it is said. Wait patiently while each parent thinks of a nice thing to say about the sculpture to the left.

A blessing is like a rolling snowball. Each of you has brought out a roll of blessing, as you have told one another good things about the foil sculptures. You each now believe you sculpt well. Blessing teenagers is like this: One word of blessing leads to confidence to try a new skill or go to a deeper level in relationships. Better skills and relationships lead to more words of blessing.

Pause to thank God for the blessing of both giving and receiving blessings.

3. How to Spur One Another On with Blessings

You'll need at least one Bible and the triangles parents created in step 2. Duplicate the five case studies. Write a sentence strip with this section of Hebrews 10:24–25: "Let us consider how we may spur one another on toward love and good deeds." Prepare to display it so there is room for the steps 4 and 5 strips.

Challenge parents to act out as many ways to cheer as they can. Suggest they pretend to be cheering at a ball game or cheering a game on television. Keep a displayed list of each variation. One parent might watch quietly, urging the team on with calm advice. Another might jump out of his chair and shout when things go great. A cheerleader might make up a poem to sing. Another parent might say "C'mon! C'mon! You can do it!" or "Go! Go! Go!"

Each of you has a slightly different style of cheering, but what is the goal of cheering?

Combine parent answers to make points such as:

- Our goal is to cheer our teenagers on as they pursue excellence.
- Our goal is to let our teenagers know we believe in them as we show them how to give their best.
- Our goal is to let our teenagers hear us say good things about their good actions.

Explain: **Christians cheering is more than just cheering our teen on; it's cheering them on toward the right actions, words, and attitudes. Hebrews 10:24–25 says it like this: "Let us consider how we may spur one another on toward love and good deeds."**

Post this sentence strip near the step 2 strip, leaving room for the step 4 part of the verse. Direct each parent to turn over the triangle of paper from step 2 and to see it like a team pennant. Challenge trios to work together to fill their pennants with cheers they can say to their teenagers, perhaps as they go off to take a test or make a new friend.

See the Bonus section below for samples in addition to these:
- *You can do it.*
- *I'm behind you all the way.*
- *I'll be cheering from here.*
- *Every game has its ups and downs. Just keep at it.*
- *I'll be watching.*
- *You're facing a tough situation. What biblical principles do you think will help?*
- *Keep using the skills we've practiced.*

Call for each parent to name a phrase that would cheer on a teen toward love and good deeds, none naming what the other has named.

Say: **Just as the blessings we gave one another at the beginning of this session gave us the confidence to sculpt with good ideas, our goal in blessing our teenagers is to draw out the good that God has created in each of our teens, and to give our teens confidence to believe and practice that good.** Pray God's specific guidance in helping parents know what to say and do to bring confidence in their teenagers.

Adaptation for a Youth-Parent Meeting

If youth are present, guide them to participate in the foil-shaping and other steps. Treat them as fully participating members of the group.

After the third or fourth step, say: **Notice that we have blessed our teenagers during this meeting by fully involving them. Sometimes simply giving teens the tasks of adult life can bless them.**

4. How to Spur One Another On with Actions

You'll need Bibles and pencils, a card, and a case study found on pages 102–106 for every parent. Write a sentence strip with this section of Hebrews 10:24–25: "And all the more as you see the Day approaching." Prepare to display it to allow room for the step 5 strip.

Say: **Words are critical. Teens have to hear us say we love them and are behind them all the way. But without coaching and skill training, words are worthless. Without skills a teen can't win in the game of life. In this step we'll name some actions through which we can coach our teens for success. Remember that "success" does not mean being the top person, but the most honorable person. I'll give you a blank card, and you write on it an area in which your teen needs to do well, to find competence.**

Provide blank cards and pens. Circulate to help, warning parents not to give identifying details. Take up these cards as they are finished. Assure parents that you will disguise them some.

Before we look at our specific situations, let's consider that most of these will apply to all of us in some form. As you listen apply the principles discovered to your own circumstances. First we'll do generic situations to get the process rolling. Give each trio of parents one of these situations with the ideas cut off and a blank card. Direct them to turn their chairs so they can work in trios. If you have more than fifteen parents, duplicate the case studies. Guide them to answer the three questions at the bottom of each case study.

School—Your teenager has so many assignments at school that he doesn't even know where to start. Some days he is panicky. Some days he acts like he doesn't care. Other days he says nothing about it.

1. What skills does a teenager need to master this circumstance?
2. Through what actions could a parent help the teen to practice?
3. What blessings might parents give during this process?

Ideas for skills to master this circumstance:
* *Time management*
* *Listing*
* *Calendaring*
* *Doing the hard tasks first and then rewarding self with the easier assignments*
* *Stick-to-it-iveness*

Through what actions parent could help:
* *Supervise so you know the work is getting done*
* *Help to separate assignments into chunks*
* *Buy an organizer that works for teen*
* *Sit with teen to keep teen going*
* *Buy ice cream or other special treat to pull out as a reward for completing a project*

Blessings:
* *"This is hard, but there are ways to do it."*
* *"This is important, so I understand why you're stressed."*
* *"If you break it down into little chunks, you can do it."*
* *"One thing at a time will whack out the whole list."*

Church—Your teenager likes Bible study but says church services are boring. Your teen wants to know if she has to do the boring stuff at church. You know that even the initially boring things can provide opportunity for interaction, for encouraging other church members, for discovering something about God, for true worship. So you want your teen to move past the hard stuff to deliver the good gifts.

1. What skills does a teenager need to master this circumstance?
2. Through what actions could a parent help the teen to practice?
3. What blessings might parents give during this process?

Ideas for skills to master this circumstance:
- *See church as a place to give and not just get*
- *Creativity to make something boring become interesting*
- *Intentionality to worship on purpose even when others don't make it easy*
- *Habit of going to church even when it doesn't seem to make any difference*

Parent could help with these actions:
- *Show how to take notes during services*
- *Show how to doodle/draw notes rather than write them*
- *Let your teen see you writing/doodling notes in worship and focusing on the songs*
- *Get teen to church just as you get teen to school*
- *Make the most of before and after worship time to encourage others*
- *Communicate church as a place to give as well as receive, explaining that we all have a spiritual gift*

Blessings:
- *"You are a critical member of the body of Christ."*
- *"I watched you learn something new through the hymns and sermon; way to focus!"*
- *"Your example helps younger youth."*
- *"Your taking up the offering is a way to encourage each person to whom you pass the plate."*

Work—Your teenager would rather watch a favorite television show than wash the dishes. (Who wouldn't?) He'd rather go to a party than go to a part-time job. You want your teen to experience and treasure the pride of a job well done for Christ's sake. You know that the party and the TV show will be happier celebrations when done after a hard day's work. You also know that work and play are part of everyone's days.

1. What skills does a teenager need to master this circumstance?
2. Through what actions could a parent help the teen to practice?
3. What blessings might parents give during this process?

Ideas for skills to master this circumstance:
- *Recognize chores and earning money as ways to love people*
- *Learn to reward self with relaxation after work rather than assume relaxation is the center of life*
- *Pride in job well done*
- *Ability to get both work and play done in the same day*

Parent could help with these actions:
- *Insist all homework and chores be done before TV, computer, or other relaxation*
- *Give no money unless earned*
- *Check work before relaxation time*
- *Show how to find time for both work and play*
- *Whistle while you work*
- *List good things mentally while working*

Blessings:
- *"I loved the way you did your chores quickly but well. Now you have more time in your day."*
- *"Work is a way to serve God. Even when flipping burgers, you can cheer up your coworkers."*
- *"Work gives a sense of accomplishment. Look how many leaves you raked!"*
- *"You did your work hours and still found time to serve at church. Way to balance life!"*

Family—Your teen uses siblings instead of loving them. Your teen borrows siblings' clothes without asking, leaves the shared bathroom a mess, says ugly things to siblings, and is just plain rude to siblings. You're convinced that siblings should treat one another better than friends because they will know one another for life. You also believe that siblings can help one another realize their strengths.

1. What skills does a teenager need to master this circumstance?
2. Through what actions could a parent help the teen practice?
3. What blessings might parents give during this process?

Ideas for skills to master this circumstance:
- *Get along with the people with whom you live*
- *Establish people habits that will make a marriage rather than break it*
- *Cooperate rather than be selfishly self-centered*
- *Use words to build up rather than tear down*

Parent could help with these actions:
- *Establish rules for borrowing and impose penalties for borrowing against the rules*
- *Provide words that talk things out respectfully*
- *See siblings as practice ground, not enemies*
- *Allow time with friends as reward for treating siblings well*

Blessings:
- *"It's hardest to be nice to the people with whom you live. Thanks for honoring God by being good to your sibling."*
- *"It's easier to snap than to talk things out. You acted like Jesus when you stayed calm."*
- *"You just built up your sister rather than bit and devoured her. Way to obey!"*

Friends—Your teen feels shy, and though you've offered your house for parties, he refuses. Your teen assumes no one would have fun at your house. Your teen chooses to stay at home rather than make plans. There's nothing wrong with a night alone once in awhile, but your teen is starting to think no one cares about him.

1. What skills does a teenager need to master this circumstance?
2. Through what actions could a parent help the teen practice?
3. What blessings might parents give during this process?

Ideas for skills to master this circumstance:
* *Party-giving*
* *Fun-having*
* *Meeting people and developing relationships*
* *Planning*
* *Spending time with people so you can experience that they enjoy you*

Parents could help with these actions:
* *Show how to give a party*
* *Shop together for some group party games such as Balderdash*
* *Have over one friend at a time to build a party group*
* *Drive groups to places so nondriving teens have a way to get there*

Blessings:
* *"I like the way you have fun with friends."*
* *"Let's have one person over this Friday."*
* *"You are such a good conversationalist."*
* *"Wow! I like the friend you chose to have over."*

Say: **Among us there is one card for each of the competencies of life: learning, serving, accomplishing, family, and friends. As we coach our teens in how to win in these areas, our cheering will have authority.**

Call on each trio to present their solutions. Pray after each that God will help us remember and apply the principles He wants.

Say: **Now I'll read the cards you wrote, one card at a time. I'm going to disguise them somewhat to make them apply to any of you. Jot down the same three actions rapidly but effectively: (1) a skill, (2) an action, and (3) a blessing through which you as a parent could impart confidence in this teen.**

Shuffle and read the situations. Provide scrap paper. After all parents have jotted an action and blessing, call on volunteers to name them. Call on a different set of volunteers each time so all parents speak at least once.

Call on a parent to read Hebrews 10:24–25, with emphasis on "and all the more as you see the Day approaching." Display this strip as you explain that our time with teens is limited to about six years. During that time God wants to work through parents to give teens confidence and competence. The "day" in this Scripture is likely the day when Jesus returns. We can also think of it as the day we no longer have daily contact with our teens.

Say: **Teens with parents who show love to them will not have to prove themselves or be prone to ridiculous challenges from people who don't love them much. As you stay deliberate about teaching skills, actions, and blessings, your teenagers will thrive. You'll have to be the heavy—insisting that siblings ask before borrowing clothes and that everyone gets chores done before going out. But by being consistent, and then expressing caring words, your teen will grow both in competence and confidence.**

Continue to explain that expressed love at home is the most powerful way to give teens a foundation for spiritual and emotional security. Comment from the introduction to this chapter.

5. Times to Bless Teens

You'll need Bibles, paper, markers, the pennants from step 2, and the final strip of Hebrews 10:24–25. Write a sentence strip with this section of Hebrews 10:24–25: "Let us not give up meeting together, as some are in the habit of doing." Prepare to display it to complete the verse.

Why should we bother to help our teens believe that they are competent by giving them skills and blessings?

Challenge the same trios to list as many reasons as they can, more than any other group.

Possibilities include:

- *Confident teenagers live their faith in God more boldly.*
- *Secure teenagers are less prone to temptation and wrong choices.*
- *Happy teenagers pick good friends and eventually a good spouse.*
- *Girls with daddies who spend time with them are less prone to guys who will use them.*
- *Hard-working teenagers demonstrate responsibility and the contentment that comes with that.*
- *Competence breeds confidence, which breeds competence, and so they build upon each other.*

Call on a parent to read Hebrews 10:24–25, with emphasis on "and all the more as you see the Day approaching."

Too many parents believe the myth that once kids get to the teen years they don't want to spend any time with parents. In truth, teens want the attention of their parents. So although this phrase applies to the church as a whole, don't forget that each family is a critical part of the church as a whole. The family is the first institution God created, and spending good time together is a great way to bless our teens and to honor God.

Challenge the same trios of parents to name times they can spend with teens both daily and for special occasions. Suggest they think first of big times to bless teens such as graduation and starting a new school year. Provide paper and markers.

Samples:

- *Starting middle school*
- *Starting any new school year*
- *Starting high school*
- *Getting driver's license*
- *Birthdays*
- *Holidays*
- *Triumphing over a hard challenge*
- *Honors nights, performances, and ball games*

Then give another set of paper and direct trios to call out times of day they might bless their teen each day. Call on the teams especially to list times they might bless their teens.

Samples include:
- *When leaving for school*
- *When arriving home from school*
- *Bedtime*
- *After a test*
- *Before a test*
- *When meeting or talking to a new friend*

Display all lists and call for parents to name a blessing they could give at one of those events, both with words and actions. Direct parents to turn their pennants back to the Scripture side and to write three times and places where they will bless their teenagers with words.

Samples:
- *As they leave in the morning—from my kitchen*
- *As they arrive home from school—via E-mail*
- *When they enter middle school—with a dinner out*
- *When they enter high school—with a dinner out*
- *Before each date—in their rooms*
- *When they face a rough challenge—with a hug*

Read in unison from the Bible, Hebrews 10:24–25 all the way through.

Adaptation For a Youth-Parent Meeting

If youth are present, before parents begin their listing, guide teens each to name a time they want to be blessed. Of course, you'll let teens know ahead of time that you'll be asking this question so they can be ready with an answer.

Time Note

If you have extra time, guide parents to write letters of blessing to their teenagers. Offer to read the letters to make certain that no hint of harshness or disdain comes through. Remind parents that letters of blessing are not secret opportunities to nag.

The Point

Make a copy of "The Point" on colored paper to give to parents.

As you give parents a copy of "The Point," invite them to name three true and encouraging adjectives they will show and tell their teen.

Sample: I'll show and tell my teen that he's brilliant, witty, and perceptive.

Allow time for all parents to do this by calculating about a minute for every two parents.

➤ The Point

Encourage with your words and validate your words with your actions.

"Let us consider how we may spur one another on toward love and good deeds. Let us not give up meeting together, as some are in the habit of doing, but let us encourage one another—and all the more as you see the Day approaching" (Heb. 10:24–25).

True confidence comes from real competence. So link words with actions. As you tell your teens you love them, show them how to be lovable by sharing the attention with siblings. When you say your teen is good company, spend time together to show him how to be good company. When you say your teen is handsome, point out his smile or another feature he can control to be handsome.

HOME DISCUSSION GUIDE

Send this page home with parents, mailing to any who were not able to attend, or mail to each parent a few days after the session as a follow-up prompter to practice "The Point."

The Point of our last parent meeting was to encourage your teen with your words and then validate your words with your actions.

Human beings need one another's encouragement every day. *"Let us consider how we may spur one another on toward love and good deeds. Let us not give up meeting together, as some are in the habit of doing, but let us encourage one another—and all the more as you see the Day approaching"* (Heb. 10:24–25).

Lay out a 100 percent cotton pillowcase and a permanent fabric marker for each of your teenagers (100 percent cotton absorbs the ink and won't fade as you wash it). Explain to your teens: "I want to let you know how much I like you. Here are some of the things I like." Write on the pillowcase at least five genuine characteristics you like in your teen. Put these at several angles and in several places on the pillowcase.

Samples:

- *I like your wit.*
- *I enjoy your company.*
- *I like the way you think things through.*
- *Talking with you about hard questions helps me see something new.*
- *You are happy.*
- *You stay invested in church.*
- *You get along with people well.*
- *You solve problems with compassion.*
- *You persist.*
- *You express your own spiritual gift of* _____
  as well as bringing out spiritual gifts in others.
- *You look out for others' needs as well as your own.*
- *You look deeply.*
- *You are not shallow.*
- *You see and say the good in people.*

Say: "What else would you like me to see in you, things I may not know you think or dream or hope for?" Listen with rapt attention as your teenager tells you thoughts, dreams, and hopes. It may start slowly and you may need to give your teen twenty-four hours to think about it. The next night insist on at least two dreams, thoughts, or hopes. Jot each thought, dream, and hope on a piece of paper; and after your teen finishes sharing, ask for phrasing to put them on the pillowcase. Choose not to put any details that would limit a dream. For example, if your teen tells about a dream to be an astronaut, you might write, "Fly one day" or "See the stars." Avoid details that could embarrass your teen whether alone or with a friend. For "I hope I'm not an old maid," you could write "Love."

Say: "Each time you snuggle down to sleep on this pillowcase, I want you to know I believe in you and in your dreams. What are some other ways you want me to show this?" You are asking this because, though you may know you love your teenager and may believe you show it very well, there may be other ways your teen wants you to express your love. Because love is a two-way thing, be willing to learn from your teen how to show love better.

Again jot these on paper. *Your teen might want to pick from a list like this:*

- *Notice what I do well rather than just harp at me when I do wrong.*
- *Tell me something new each day that you like.*
- *Show me how to change rather than just tell me to change.*
- *Listen, just listen, rather than jump in and tell me what to do. I want to make my own smart choices.*
- *Practice what you preach.*
- *Help me with my stress!*
- *Show me what to do about* _____.

NEWSLETTER IDEA

Use these as a base for a parent newsletter, for youth-written articles, or for the parent section of the church newsletter.

How to Enjoy a Teenager in Seven Easy Steps

Don't fall prey to the rumors that teenagers are trouble or are hard to live with. Everybody is trouble and hard to live with, at least from time to time. Living with people is hard; that's why it's so hard to make a marriage work. But as we choose to do the considerate thing and choose to show loving actions, we will get along and enjoy one another. As your teenagers become adults, they'll make more and more choices to get along with people (or not to do so). Show them how to pick the former by practicing on your own family. With such steady guidance at home, they'll love people more consistently and build happier relationships.

Step 1—Go somewhere with few people around. State parks, hiking trails, out-of-town museums, and your car are good beginning spots. When no one is around to see them, teenagers let down their guard and enjoy themselves more freely.

Step 2—Tease in ways that build up your teen, never in ways that put him down. "Uh-oh, two girls are coming down the trail. I have to hide you so your good looks don't overwhelm them. I don't want some girl stealing my good-looking son."

Step 3—Do together whatever you're doing. Walk the trail. Set up the picnic. Start the fire. Share the binoculars. Spot the rare bird. Shared adventures lead to genuine closeness.

Step 4—Notice and speak out loud the good things your teenager does. "I notice that you keep a steady pace when you hike rather than rush and then rest. That's good use of your energy."

Step 5—Make them do it. Your teens will complain and claim that no one else's parents make them go on nature hikes, that they outgrew that long ago. But make them go anyway. They'll end up enjoying themselves and will ask when they can go again.

Step 6—Stay majorly cool if anyone approaches. Get quiet. Stop the silliness. Act calm. Your teen's reputation is at stake.

Step 7—Repeat the processes in your own kitchen or garage. When it's just you and your teen, you can tease, do things together, notice, and coerce. And you'll enjoy togetherness each day.

Parents who genuinely like their teenagers, and let them know it, give those teenagers a rock-solid base of security and joy. They will always know that their parents loved them.

E-MAIL IDEAS

Choose from these parent-support ideas, tips, and strategies especially for electronic transmission. (Remember: Don't create an E-mail Elite; print out and mail the messages to any parents who don't have E-mail).

Teens liking themselves is a God-esteem thing, not a self-esteem thing. Because God has made each teenager and because He shows each teenager how to choose well and do well, teens can choose to live the worth God has created in them. They can love themselves as a basis for loving others. To help your teens believe their God-imparted worth:

- Give attention. Ignoring your teens makes them feel invisible. Listen with rapt attention to their stories to impart power to solve a problem, stop a wrong, start a good, or celebrate a happy experience.
- Spend time. Your schedule is likely so busy you can't even list all you have to do. Write in your day-planner time to spend with your teenager. Make an appointment to go out to eat, take a walk, work on the car, whatever the two of you like to do.
- Notice. Tell your teen the Christlike actions you see her do: "I saw you

show love when you . . ." Then repeat when you see instances of joy, peace, patience, kindness, goodness, faithfulness, gentleness, and self-control (Gal. 5:22–23).

- Bless. Give your teen a blessing to start each day such as: "I know you can do it." "I'll be praying for you." "I'll look forward all day to hearing the events of your day." (See the Bonus section for more examples.)
- Thank. At the end of each day, invite your teen to tell you the good God brought into his day. Together you can thank God for that good gift.

And if you're sending the E-mail to a cell phone, here's a short one: You and your teenager are valuable because God made you.

WHAT TEENAGERS WANT PARENTS TO KNOW

Choose from these questions that invite your teens to share with you anonymous quotes, quips, and comments via E-mail or anonymous survey. Feel free to choose one question at a time as the "Question of the Week."

I'll combine your ideas with no names or identifying details to distribute to parents. Feel free to answer a question that's not here or to suggest another question for everyone to answer:

- Even though we know God made us and that what God made is good, most people have an incredibly difficult time liking themselves. Why do you think this is true?
- Through what actions do your parents let you know that they like you or enjoy you?
- Through what words do your parents let you know that they like you or enjoy you? (Tell exact quotes.)
- What other loving actions and loving words do you wish your parents would give to you?
- Tell about a time you know you were totally loved.
- What strategies help you believe the good God has created in you?

TROUBLESHOOTING

Suggest these actions to implement when a teen does not display the expected behavior.

Suppose that no matter what you do, your teen still has trouble liking herself.

- Practice together the tasks of life: time management, getting along with people, solving problems, learning tough subjects, doing church well, expressing responsibility, fixing mistakes. With competence comes confidence.

- Find a skill your teen has and feed it. If your teen is artistic, buy an easel and paints. If your teen shows sensitivity, volunteer together at a homeless shelter. If your teen reads avidly, find good books and magazines. If your teen mows lawns well, help start a lawn-mowing business.

- Especially if your teen has communicated trouble liking self to you, explain that every human struggles with liking self. Suggest: "Press on through the struggle to daily tell yourself one good thing you see in yourself, so you can daily come closer to believing the good God created in you."

- Regularly spend time with each of your teens. Let your teen draw on your strength—strength you have drawn from God.

Bonus Idea

This idea is a starter list of blessings so you can use your words and actions to bless your teen.

Possible way to use: Reduce, print, and laminate to make a wallet card. Explain that the genuine blessing of parents is the most powerful foundation for healthily loving others as we love ourselves. Give each parent a copy of this wallet card. Remember to mail one to each parent, two to some homes, one to each of two homes in other cases.

A Dozen Blessings to Give Your Teen

Give your teenagers the power to love others in godly ways (including themselves) by giving daily a genuine blessing. Some samples to get you going:

1. "You kept with it until you mastered that challenge. Good persistence."
2. "Living with you is fun."
3. "You let self-control triumph over temper. Way to honor God."
4. "I love hearing what you think."
5. "Tell me your dream."

6. "You live like Jesus when you _____." *(Sample: firmly but kindly share your point; stop the cycle of evil by refusing revenge)*
7. "Watch for the blessing God pokes into this day. I'll be waiting to hear about it."
8. "That was a brilliant solution to that problem."
9. "I like spending time with you."
10. "Reading and thinking led you to this point. Way to evaluate for yourself!"
11. "That was mature behavior. I'm impressed."
12. "You're choosing what to do rather than letting life happen to you. Way to seize the blessing!"

CHAPTER 7

They're Getting Too Serious

So protect them emotionally, sexually, and spiritually.

"I don't like the boy my daughter is dating, but if I ask too many questions or prohibit this, she will probably want to date him all the more."

"I can tell that my son likes girls, but he never asks them out. I guess the girls are going to have to ask him."

Dating is the area into which most parents are least likely to venture, and yet it's the area where teenagers need the most help.

"Why do I feel this about her?"

"Does he like me?"

"Am I in love?"

"How far is too far?"

"How can I get a boyfriend and keep him?"

"What if I call her and she turns me down?"

These questions are more than just adolescent angst, though they are certainly that. Answers to questions about dating and love determine what kind of person a teen will marry and what kind of family that couple will establish for generations. Getting to know the opposite sex is more than just a what-will-I-do-on-Friday-night question. It's a question of heritage and living out (or turning against) God's plan for their lives.

Goal—This chapter guides parents to teach their teens how to get to know good people of the opposite sex and, more specifically, how to fulfill the powerful yearning for lifelong love with a godly marriage partner.

PARENT WORKSHOP

Draw from these ideas to lead a one-hour parent workshop.

1. Move from Worry to Friendships

You'll need a Bible, paper, markers, and a ballpoint pen for each parent. Arrange the chairs in two circles and prepare instruction posters for both teams. If you have more than twenty parents, create duplicate teams. Consider duplicating an outline of a hand for those who prefer that to writing on their own hand.

As parents enter, send them to one of two teams: (1) Those born on even days go to the first group. (2) Those born on odd days go to the second group. Provide paper and markers to both groups. Challenge the even group:

List all the potential problems caused by a teen who dates too early or too often. Include problems from the constantly dating extreme all the way to the center of the spectrum of going out occasionally and healthily.

Samples:
- *May date people much older, which creates such problems as sexual temptation and widely different life experiences*
- *May want to go further and further sexually with each date*
- *Having once had a steady relationship, may believe must always have one*
- *May cut off other friends of both sexes to focus on the one guy/girl relationship*
- *May stop concentrating on school*
- *May stay with someone who doesn't mature at the same rate*
- *May pick people who don't really match later in life*
- *May miss other critical life skills for that age*
- *May get pregnant*
- *May get someone else pregnant*
- *May contract sexually transmitted disease*
- *May change personality to match the beloved*
- *May jump from person to person and then have trouble committing later*

Challenge the second group:

List all the potential problems caused by a teen who stays home on weekend nights or a teen who has few or no dates. Include problems all the way to the center of the spectrum of going out occasionally and healthily.

Samples:
- *May become so lonely that will fall for the affections of someone with not-so-pure motives.*
- *May grow to believe that he is not likable. There's nothing wrong with not having dates, but there is something wrong with staying isolated.*
- *As long as going out in groups, there is little to worry about.*
- *Isolation may lead to missing the guys and girls God wants them to know.*
- *Isolation keeps teens from developing their guy-relating and girl-relating skills.*
- *An occasional date brings light to this situation, but teens may feel extra pressure to keep that relationship going.*
- *Not dating can free teens to focus on other life skills, but they may not see this as an advantage.*
- *Even with a good dating relationship, there are sexual pressures.*
- *Hard to balance dating with other friendships and with school.*
- *May feel like a loser.*

Circulate and feed samples to both groups to ensure that all ranges of problems are listed.

Call for groups to present their lists in a lighthearted, humorous way. Prompt one side to name a problem from its list, and then prompt the other side to argue back by choosing a problem from its list and begin with "My teen's problem is worse than your teen's problem because . . ." Then prompt the first team to argue back by naming another problem after claiming, "My teen's problem is worse than your teen's problem because . . ." Stress that these are not the actual problems of the speaker's teen, and that even amidst the problems there are always places to be thankful. For example, the teen at home on a Friday can rest and refresh for the next week. The teen out on a Friday can enjoy the togetherness that comes from a good relationship.

Teaching Tip

Why bother with getting parents to argue good-naturedly with one another about which problem is "worse"? Why not just say, "No matter what your teen's age and level of dating comfort, there are problems and advantages," and be done with it? Because parents, like teens, suffer silently over matters of romance. They worry and wonder whether anyone will love their teens for a lifetime and if their teens will choose good people to love them. As they look around, they conclude that no one else has it as rough as they do. This arguing process helps them grasp that all teens, and parents, struggle. They find some relief in the fact that at least they don't have all the problems at the same time.

After several minutes of good-natured arguing, stress:

As you have skillfully pointed out, there are definite problems all over the dating spectrum, from those who date too much and too early to those who fear they will never get a date to those who date at good ages and in good amounts. Rather than fret and worry, we parents must take deliberate action.

Our teens weren't born knowing how to date, how to meet girls, or how to respond to guys. So we must teach them. Should parents panic if teens don't have a date on Friday nights? Of course not. Teens may not date until well into their college years or their twenties. But we must show them how to build guy-girl relationships no matter what their current ages. Relating includes both friendships and romantic relationships. In fact, the friendships tend to build the strongest bonds for marriage. Because God instituted the home as the center of spiritual training, we parents must help our teens discover what real love is—a set of actions based on godly virtues—and show them how to express that love. And we must coach them in the art of calling, dating, courtship—whatever we want to label the process of approaching and getting to know someone romantically.

The yearning for the opposite sex is more than something fathers worry about with their daughters. It's godly, God-given, and designed to be guided by God. The establishment of love relationships is second in importance only to your teen's relationship with God Himself. So recognize it, bless it, and show your teens how to express it.

Yes, there will be red faces.

Yes, there will be dangers along the way.

Yes, there will be fervent claims of "I already know this!"

But there will also be secret relief when you go ahead and teach anyway. Much pain will be saved when you refuse to let them date unhealthy people. There will be happy faces when good friendships turn into lifelong marriages. And solid love will be created and passed down to the next generation.

Distribute ballpoint pens and encourage parents to write on their five fingers these five single-word ways to teach love skills that we will study during this session. Offer the option of jotting the five on a paper hand for any who are uncomfortable writing on their hands. Comment on each while they add these to their hands.

1. *Know*

   What you want to teach, such as the fact that God is the author of love and that qualities such as love, joy, peace, patience, kindness, goodness, gentleness, faithfulness, and self-control are the most romantic of all. You'll also want to teach that because the yearning for love is so strong, it is fraught with dangers. God will help us avoid these as we choose deliberately to pick and to grow close to the best people.

2. *Converse*

   This is different from lecturing or just listening but includes the best of both. It is a true exchange between you and your teen that leads to understanding.

3. *Pray*

   Prayer is at the center of all five actions, so we put it on the central finger. Pray that God will show you what to teach, how to teach it, and when to teach it. He will generously do both.

4. *Attention*

   Give generous amounts of it at home. Teens who are loved well at home, and know it, are much less likely to turn to unhealthy romances. If they do, they don't stay in that relationship.

5. *Affection*

   Show teens how to give it, how to receive it, and how much is just right for dating relationships. Rather than say, "Set your limits," explain specifically what those limits should be.

2. Know What You Want to Teach

You'll need Bibles, scratch paper and markers to write ideas, and copies of the four team assignments. Print the team assignments, duplicating them if you have more than twelve parents. Prepare to sketch a large hand silhouette.

The first thing to decide is what to teach our teens. What is love and what actions make love grow?

Divide the two parent teams into two more teams each, and give each team one of these assignments. If you have fewer than eight parents, form teams of two and choose from the assignments. Assure parents that each team has some sort of singing or talking part, so though all will be acting silly, all will do it together. Stress that the goal is to remember characteristics of love and that singing helps us do that.

Team 1—Write a song to the tune of "Jesus Loves Me" that teaches the love qualities listed in Galatians 5:22–23. You may include as many verses as you want, but you must include each of the nine expressions of godly love (commonly known as the fruit of the Holy Spirit). Everyone in your group must present your song.

Team 2—Create a commercial of the "if you act now, we'll also throw in steak knives" type to advertise the benefit of all the actions in 1 Corinthians 13:4–7. You must include all the love qualities, perhaps starting with the one teens will like best and why it's worth spending their lives on. Then throw in all the other qualities of love one at a time, explaining why they are desired. Everyone in your group must present your commercial.

Team 3—Create a cheer that illustrates the Philippians 2:4 way to win at love: "Look not only to your own interests, but also to the interests of others." You must include the entire verse in your cheer, but you can break it down into phrases. Be certain to communicate that both people in a relationship must live by this verse or one will end up using the other. Everyone in your group must present the cheer.

Team 4—Write a new verse to a familiar hymn or a wedding song that celebrates God's plan for each person to leave the family of origin and cleave to a spouse with the goal of creating a new family. Quote Genesis 2:24 as part of your wedding song. Stress the value of waiting until marriage for cleaving, and include a verse on how to wait until marriage for the leaving and cleaving. Everyone in your group must present the hymn.

Call for each team to sing its song/commercial/cheer/hymn. Prompt generous support from the group for the performers. Rejoice by saying:

Say: **God has created a great gift in the opposite sex. There is much good to be enjoyed in dating and in marriage and in a lifetime together** with a good life mate. **Let's thank Him for this.** Invite each person to add a single sentence. Close by inviting His guidance as we show our teens how to live well God's intentions for this relationship.

What was your comfort level in writing and presenting your song?

Jot on a chalkboard ratings from one to ten as parents call them out. Explain:

Some of us were uncomfortable, similar to our teens who are uneasy entering guy-girl relationships. They know it can be fun but fear they will blow it. These teens may avoid guy-girl relationships rather than risk rejection. Or they may let someone else do the courting, taking whoever comes along, rather than actively seek God's best.

Invite brief comparisons between parents' discomfort in writing and singing songs and teen's choices in guy-girl relationships.

Some of us were comfortable and took on the challenge with gusto, similar to the way our teens go after guy-girl relationships with gusto.

Invite brief comparisons between parents' comfort in writing and singing songs and teen's choices in guy-girl relationships.

Whether initially comfortable or not, we parents created beautiful music. This is our goal in guiding teens through their dating relationships, that they work with God to create beautiful friendships and eventually a contented marriage.

Sketch a quick hand silhouette on a chalkboard or poster and fill in "Know" and "Pray" on the fingers to indicate that this step addressed these.

3. Converse

You'll need Bibles and the sketch of the hand begun in step 2. See chapter 3 for more ideas.

Fill in the "Converse" finger on the hand to indicate that this step will address the give-and-take of good conversations as a way to teach about dating.

Say: **Conversing includes the give-and-take we share with our teenagers every day. As we talk regularly with our teens, we can teach about how to approach a guy or girl, how to let someone know you care, how to ask for or accept a date, and so much more. Remember, nobody's born knowing how to do these things, and because God has entrusted us with the raising of our teens, we are the best ones to teach this.**

- What's the difference between *conversing* and *lecturing*?
- What's the difference between *lecturing* and *actual learning*?

Await many responses for each question.

Gather all adults into one group by guiding them to move their chairs into a single circle. Guide each adult around the circle to name something they could say in casual conversation to teach one of the step 2 truths that were sung (or another Bible teaching about love). Urge none to say what any other has said. To make it especially challenging, direct parents to repeat all the statements the other parents have said before adding theirs. This may make some parents so anxious they don't focus on what they want to say, so assess your group.

Samples:

- *"Yes, those are cute boys walking there. Aren't you glad God created guys?" (Teaches Gen. 2:23–24.)*
- *"Oh my, she is a good piece of God's work! God did well when He created women." (Teaches Gen. 2:23–24.)*
- *"When you telephone her to ask her out, impress her by showing interest in her, not by boasting or strutting or bragging." (Teaches 1 Cor. 13:4–7).*
- *"She doesn't call all the attention to herself, and yet she's willing to share her opinion. You've found a keeper there." (Teaches Phil. 2:4.)*
- *"He works hard and yet makes certain he has time for his own family, for church, and for coming over here. That's a good balance between his interests and the interests of others." (Teaches Phil. 2:4.)*
- *"His going to places you like to go as well as inviting you to places he likes to go shows that he is not self-seeking. Very cool." (Teaches 1 Cor. 13:4–7.)*
- *"Your friend Roy is such a kind man. Way to be a manly man like Jesus!" (Teaches Gal. 5:22–23.)*
- *"You're smart to spend time with Lesley because she is good to you and to other people as well." (Teaches Gal. 5:22–23.)*

Say: **We parents tend to overtalk in our teaching. So aim to keep your dating teaching in one sentence per talk. If you teen talks back or asks a question, you can add another sentence, but avoid the lecture mode.**

Invite parents briefly to tell ways they keep from overtalking or undertalking. Humorously limit each parent to one sentence to illustrate the point. Agree that it's tough to talk succinctly, but a pithy point is accepted more easily than a verbose one.

3. Converse to Work Out Details

You'll need Bibles, a chalkboard or poster, masking tape, and the sketch of the hand begun in step 2.

Say: **Conversing to drop in bits of wisdom is one of the fun parts of parenting. A not-as-fun part is also important: the working out of dating guidelines for your household.**

Write these examples on the chalkboard or a poster as groups share them.

Say: **For example, How old must your teen be to date? Will the dates occur mainly in your home as in courtship? Why will you meet the dates first? How much chaperoning by you or others will you require? What other examples do you have?**

Samples parents might choose include:
- *How to keep a dating relationship healthy.*
- *How to keep from withdrawing from friends and family when dating.*
- *How to, and how often to, supervise dating teens.*
- *How to keep teens from getting too serious too soon.*
- *How to approach dating as a godly pursuit, second in importance only to the yearning for God.*
- *How to choose the quality of person you would marry even if you're not of marriageable age.*
- *How to settle for the best and not throw your pearls before pigs (Matt. 7:6).*
- *How to tell if the differences are natural or dangerous.*
- *How to walk through the "I'll never get a date!" years.*

Invite adults to choose one of the dating guidelines and tell in three sentences or less how they handle or could handle it in their homes.

Examples:

For how to supervise dating teens:
- *No matter how much my teen bucks, there will always be an adult in the home when he is with a date.*
- *Even the strongest teenager will be tempted sexually; I will expect my dating teens to plan all dates so that time alone is brief but meaningful.*

- *Because Christians are among those having sex and getting pregnant, I will stay nearby to keep my teen from becoming one of those by accident.*

For how to choose the quality of person you would marry:

- *If you already know the person is not a Christian or a Christian who doesn't live according to the Bible, don't date that person.*
- *Once you discover that your values and commitments are different, choose to date someone else.*
- *Stress that even if "just dating," we get attached to people, so always date only people you would marry.*

 Time Note

These dating topics are the kinds of issues that could take an entire session all by themselves. By limiting to three sentences, you touch on tough issues without getting bogged down in them. Explain this to parents.

4. Converse to Work Out the Approach

You'll need Bibles, masking tape, four signs, and the sketch of the hand begun in step 2. Post on the four walls these signs: Courtship, Dating, Going Out in Groups, Seeing People in Regular Life Such as School and Bible Studies.

One of the big debates in recent years is whether dating is actually the best way to get to know people of the opposite sex. Courtship has been proposed as an alternative, as have other options. Let's converse about this briefly with a walking discussion.

Point out on the four walls these signs:

- Courtship
- Dating
- Going out in groups
- Seeing people in regular life such as school and Bible studies

Then ask these questions and direct parents to walk to the one they believe best answers that need and be prepared to give the reason. Insist that all parents walk to a sign before calling on any of the parents. Call on one or two in each group, varying whom you call on so that you call on everyone about the same amount.

Samples:

- *Growing a guy-girl relationship can be tense. The approach that would give the most comfort and naturalness is _____ because . . .*

- *You don't marry the person; you marry the family. For this reason _____ would be the best way to grow a guy-girl relationship because . . .*
- *Seeing how the person behaves in regular life is the best predictor of a happy relationship. For this reason _____ would be the best way to grow a guy-girl relationship because . . .*
- *Though each approach has its strengths, I like _____ because . . .*
- *_____ takes priority over _____ because . . .*
- *_____ and _____ are about the same because . . .*
- *Sexual pressures are best managed with _____ because . . .*
- *Because the person a teen meets in high school could become a spouse, I favor _____.*

Call on a different person at each sign, varying whom you call on so each parent speaks about equally.

Discuss as needed with questions like these:

- **How will you implement the many-faceted wisdom of this discussion into your own teen's life?**
- **How can you take advantage of all four strategies?**

5. Give Attention So Your Teens Know What Real Love Is

You'll need Bibles, pens, the sketch of the hand begun in step 2, and for each parent a three-by-five-inch card.

Add *attention* and *prayer* to the hand silhouette on a chalkboard or poster to indicate that this step addresses these.

Say: **Teens who know they are loved at home much less frequently turn to unhealthy romances; and if they do, they don't stay in that relationship because it doesn't measure up to the true love they've experienced at home. Loving your teen is not the same as your teen knowing you love him or her. Your teen must experience and believe that love. What do you do to give your teen regular attention? Write on your card at least three ways you make certain your teen knows you love him or her.**

Gather parents into their step 2 groups to tell one another a story of one of the ways they wrote on their cards.

Samples:

- *"I take each of my daughters out on a fast-food dinner date once a week, each by herself. I listen to the events of her week and ask lightly, 'Is there anything about which you'd like my vast wisdom?' Because I try not to make my answers any longer than three sentences, I think they ask more often."*

- *"My son and I do the dishes every night after supper. I want him to know that chores are not women's work, and I also want him to have my undivided attention. No one but us is allowed in the kitchen during this time."*
- *"I ride with my teen to church even though he's driving. Our church is quite a distance from our home, and the twenty minutes in the car lets me hear about school before church and youth group after church."*
- *"I make certain my teen does the right thing. When my teen accuses me of being mean, I explain that if I didn't care I would let her do whatever she wanted. But because I love her, I want her happy."*

Circulate to encourage groups. Call for volunteers to share a story (with permission) from a member of their group that they believe would encourage the whole group. Then allow a moment for them to get this permission. The reason for letting another share the stories is that it keeps the individuals from feeling like they're bragging.

Thank parents for treasuring their teens enough to spend time with them, and encourage them to keep finding new ways to do this.

General attention is the foundation, but we cannot stop there. We also have to provide the attention that supervises. Don't let your teens be in the house with a date unless an adult is present. Don't allow dates that are not planned. Know the people your teens date. Do not allow your teen to date people who are not good for them.

Tell a story about Earl, the boy who was the moral center of the youth group. Because his parents let him spend afternoons at his girlfriend's house (he had taken the True Love Waits pledge), he and his girlfriend got pregnant the summer they graduated from high school. He lost his college scholarship and the education of his dreams.

Say: **How would supervision have helped? What other supervision approaches do you practice?**

Stress that through prayer God will show us what supervision to give and how to manage the other aspects of guiding our children to date and marry well. Repeat that like an umbrella, all the actions radiate from the center of communication with God. Pray that parents will guide their teens as God would, prodding them on toward goodness while passionately caring about each detail of their lives.

What else would God do for our teens if He were their parent?
Stress that God is like a parent to our teens and to us.

6. Give Affection at Home and Teach Dating Affection

You'll need Bibles, the instruction poster, and the sketch of the hand begun in step 2. Prepare the instruction poster in three parts—a blank part to write ideas, instructions to add to it, and the ideas.

Fill in *affection* on the hand silhouette on a chalkboard or poster to indicate that this step addresses these.

Say: **Though affection from a parent is different from affection from a date, hugs from parents give youth the physical touch they need to stay emotionally and relationally stable. Think of it as "rubber band bonding"—you're giving your teen closeness while giving freedom to venture out and grow relationships with others.**

What do you want your teens to know about affection on dates before marriage?

Jot parental ideas on a poster and then use parent comments to stress:

Say: **Our goal is to guide our teens to choose sexual purity. Good Christians are among those who get pregnant every year. They don't mean to become as physically involved as they do; they just don't want to spoil the romantic moment. As you encourage teens to see sex as a good gift from our very good God, show them how to preserve it for marriage.**

Add these instructions to the poster:

> Talking about physical affection with our teens can be really embarrassing. But if we don't do the teaching, folks who don't have our teens' best interest in mind will. Though face-to-face communication is important, written communication can supplement our teaching and guiding. Let's prepare instruction booklets, writing on each page one helpful hint for your teen to express affection lovingly to a date.

Give each parent a small spiral notebook (available for under a dollar at discount stores), and challenge them to create as a team "Rules for Affection" notebooks. Encourage parents to make the notebooks similar to those of their team, even identical, but to customize their notebooks for their own specific teens. Parents may want to keep some pages private. The reason for the spiral-bound notebook is so parents can tear out a page if they don't like it and so they can add more ideas in later weeks and months. An alternative is to fold paper three times in half to create a small, sixteen-page booklet. Staple the spine and cut apart the pages.

Post these ideas on a computer-generated display or the instruction poster, suggesting parents do two pages for each, with an idea on each page. If they have a spiral-bound notebook, they can do even more pages for each:

1. List simple romantic things that make dates feel cared for, such as a single kiss at the end of a date, holding hands during a movie, bumping shoulders occasionally, squeezing a hand and letting go.

2. Tell about treasuring the little affections rather than having to do more and more on each date.

3. Explain that sex is a gift from God and there is no need to be ashamed of these feelings. But just as fire is better in the fireplace, sex is best in marriage. Show how to plan dates so teens don't end up with nothing to do but kiss and hug.

4. Name the limits you recommend so teens know how far is too far. "You'll know" is not enough. Example: No hands where a swimsuit goes.

5. Suggest ways to be physically polite to others when with a date. For example, include people around you in your conversations rather than smooch in the corner.

6. Lines and feelings can be powerful. Show your teen how to outsmart these while still looking cool and romantic. Example: "If you love me, you'll let me" can be countered with "If you love me, you won't make me."

7. Write a letter to each of your teens telling why you want him or her to give virginity as a wedding gift.

8. List tips for looking forward to sexual expression in marriage.

In all your pages communicate why you want the best for your teenager.

Invite parents to tell one page of their books that they won't mind other parents copying for their books. Allow a pause between each report so parents can copy it into their books. Continually as parents report, stress:

Say: **Love is a series of choices. You are showing your teens how to choose love and how to choose people who will choose to love them.**

If you plan to use it, promise parents:

There will be a newsletter article coming called "Develop a Dating Instruction Book" that will help you expand your dating book to all areas

of dating. If any of you have ideas for this, feel free to give them to me and I'll include them in the newsletter article.

See starter copy below under "Develop a Dating Instruction Book."

 ## Adaptation for a Youth-Parent Meeting

If youth are present, put a youth on each team to help create the dating and affection instruction booklet. Don't put them on the same team with their own parent to cut down on either one becoming embarrassed.

The Point

Make a copy of "The Point" on colored paper to give to parents. Display the completed sketch of the hand begun in step 2.

As you distribute copies of "The Point," review the five ways to teach love skills by prompting all parents to hold up their hands, and five different parents tell you one of the points and briefly explain how to do it.

1. Know *(what God wants you to teach)*
2. Converse *(different from lecture or just listening but a true exchange that leads to understanding)*
3. Pray *(This is at the center of action. God will generously show you what to teach and how to teach it)*
4. Attention *(both for your teen and given during dating to help your teen manage)*
5. Affection *(show teens how to give it, how to receive it, and how much is just right for dating relationships)*

Then call on a preenlisted guest youth to put his hand in the hand of his parent and say: "Hand in hand. That's how we teenagers want you to teach us." Then say something like: "Enjoy sharing life and love with your teenagers."

 ## Adaptation for a Youth-Parent Meeting

If youth are present, guide each one to go to their parents and put their hands in the hands of their parents. If any are there without their parents or teens, create a large circle of youth-parent-youth-parent so all have a hand to hold.

➤ The Point

Guide your teenagers to notice and go after qualities of godliness in their guy-girl relationships while they develop those qualities in themselves:

"The fruit of the Spirit is love, joy, peace, patience, kindness, goodness, faithfulness, gentleness and self-control. Against such things there is no law" (Gal. 5:22–23).

Growing a love relationship happens with deliberate actions rather than what's commonly known as "falling in love." Show your teens how to meet, spend time with, recognize character in, and grow deeper relationships with the best dates.

HOME DISCUSSION GUIDE

Send this page home with parents, mailing to any who were not able to attend, or mail to each parent a few days after the session as a follow-up prompter to practice "The Point."

The Point of our last parent meeting was to guide your teenagers to notice and go after qualities of godliness while they develop those qualities in themselves.

Love is built, not found. Passages like Galatians 5:22–23 show qualities of a godly boyfriend or girlfriend: *"The fruit of the Spirit is love, joy, peace, patience, kindness, goodness, faithfulness, gentleness, and self-control."*

The best guys and girls are not cute ones or even the ones that go to your church. They're the ones who show in their lives that God makes a difference. Together with your teen take turns naming ways a boyfriend/girlfriend should express each fruit of the Holy Spirit.

Examples:

- *They show love by treating every person as though that person is the last one on earth.*
- *They show joy by delighting in simple things like raindrops and rainbows.*
- *They cultivate peace by finding what they can do about a problem rather than simply fretting about it.*
- *They show patience by choosing to wait rather than whine, recognizing patience as a choice and not a feeling.*

- *They show kindness by taking turns and evenly splitting the last piece of marvelous chocolate cake.*
- *They show goodness by giving their best effort even when no one is looking.*
- *They show faithfulness by standing up for friends and standing firm for what Jesus would champion.*
- *They gently care about children, parents, themselves, and the one they date through showing genuine interest.*
- *They exercise self-control over things that hinder them, whether shyness or talking too much.*

Challenge your teenager to find you expressing each of these nine fruit of the Holy Spirit within a week's time. Explain that you will simultaneously watch for them to show the same nine fruits. The first one to catch the other doing all nine wins a dinner out purchased by the other (agree on the restaurant ahead of time).

This accomplishes three purposes:

1. Your teen learns to recognize qualities of godliness; he or she then can recognize them in potential dates.
2. Your teen learns deliberately to express qualities of godliness; he or she can then choose to show those qualities in his or her dating relationships.
3. Your teen discovers that families can choose to love one another; he or she can then choose true love with his or her own spouse and children.

Communicate repeatedly and in a variety of ways that growing a love relationship happens with deliberate actions rather than what's commonly known as "falling in love." Show your teens how to meet, spend time with, recognize character in, and grow deeper relationships with the best dates.

NEWSLETTER IDEA

Use these as a base for a parent newsletter, for youth-written articles, or for the parent section of the church newsletter.

Develop a Dating Instruction Book

Together with your teenagers develop a dating manual. You might use a tiny three-ring notebook to which you can add and take out pages. Distribute the pages among you, your spouse, and your teen.

Some content to add to your manual:

- Draw honorable "plays." Let these be similar to the way a coach places *X*s on a field and shows where they must move. Create some for several dating scenarios: meeting, talking for the first time, going on a casual date, going on a more formal date.
- Manners that girls love—opening doors, putting on her coat, letting her take your arm. Sketch or describe these. Consider practicing these skills with light humor.
- Manners guys love—letting them pick, saying you're glad they called, making them feel comfortable when they call.
- Manners everybody likes—paying attention to you even when there are other people around, saving kisses for private moments rather than making others feel like a fifth wheel, including others in conversations.
- Ways to pick good dates.
  1. Date your best friends. They're the most fun dates and marriage partners.
  2. Like the person yourself rather than let friends sway you. Do your own choosing.
  3. Parents, siblings, and good friends are your best sources of whether someone is a good match for you. You can always find someone who says your date is good or bad, but the people who know and love you best will be your most accurate.
  4. Watch out for matchmakers. Though there are honorable ones, too many people say, "You look good together," because it's risk-free for them to play with your relationship.

5. Be true to God, true to yourself, and true to the one you date.
6. HINT: Draw from the eleven tips in the BONUS section of this chapter.

- Warning signs that someone is not a good match for you—closed subjects (when you bring them up he gets mad or sad or quiet), hiding from your family, a bad temper (many people have a temper they control; those who can't control their tempers spell danger), lack of work ethic, wanting you to pay attention to them exclusively.
- Encouraging signs that someone is a good match for you—freedom to talk about anything, makes you want to live your faith more intensely, works hard at school, works hard at jobs or volunteer work, brings out in you good parts of yourself you never noticed, you get along with everyone better.

E-MAIL IDEAS

Choose from these parent-support ideas, tips, and strategies especially for electronic transmission. (Remember: Don't create an E-mail Elite; print out and mail the messages to any parents who don't have E-mail).

Consider sending your teen E-mail messages with love advice in them. Sometimes electronic information is more digestible. Say something like: "I realize I'm a parent, but believe it or not, I do remember a bit about love. In fact, I'm still growing a love relationship with Mama (or Daddy, if Mama is speaking). Here is something I've learned: . . ."

You can tell if someone is compatible with you if she is close to your age, values the same things and experiences, brings out the best in you, and is at the same place as you are life-experience wise.

Enjoying the simple things and sharing the stuff of life (like homework and chores and going to school) is more romantic than the best candlelight dinner.

The little things mean the most: someone who listens to you, someone who talks to you, someone with whom you can relax.

A guy (girl) who shows love, joy, peace, patience, kindness, goodness, faithfulness, gentleness, and self-control is more attractive than any physical beauty. In fact, those things make her good-looking.

And if you're sending the E-mail to a cell phone, here's a short one: The more alike you are, the better you are to date. "Opposites attract" applies to magnets not people.

WHAT TEENAGERS WANT PARENTS TO KNOW

Choose from these question that invite your teens to share with you anonymous quotes, quips, and comments via E-mail or anonymous survey. Feel free to choose one question at a time as the "Question of the Week."

I'll combine your ideas with no names or identifying details to distribute to parents. Feel free to answer a question that's not here or to suggest another question for everyone to answer:

- What's one thing your parents understand about guy-girl relationships?
- Do you find it easier to talk to your dad or mom about dating or about liking someone? Why?
- Why do you think so many people go too far sexually? What could parents do to help prevent this?
- What commitments have you already made to save sex until marriage? Why do you want to be a virgin until you marry?
- What's a rule in your house, or a friend's house, that helps teenagers make the right choices of who to date and what to do on those dates?
- What do you like about your parents' marriage? How will you make sure your marriage is even better?

TROUBLESHOOTING

Suggest these actions to implement when a teen does not display the expected behavior.

Suppose no matter what you've done, your teen has chosen an unhealthy dating relationship. You'll have to supervise even more.

Examples:

- Do not allow them to go out more than once a month, if that often. Doing this allows your teen to build relationships with other people, out of sheer boredom if nothing else.
- Physically supervise your teen so you make certain your teen doesn't sneak out or secretly rendezvous with this person. You may have to go so far as physically tying your wrists to your teen's while sleeping.

- Continue to explain why your teen is a treasure and why you want your teen treasured (why you don't want your teen to throw his pearls before swine, Matt. 7:6).

Bonus Idea

This idea is a guide for teaching your teen to be a good date.

Possible way to use: Enlarge, print on parchment-looking paper, and distribute to all youth parents. Use in a discussion or over an E-mail forum as: How is teaching your teen to date like eating a multicourse dinner?

Guide Your Teen to Be a Good Date

Teens aren't born knowing how to meet and charm dates. To keep them from getting their notions of romance from not-so-honest sources, proactively teach your teen to date. Some things to say and do:

1. "Love is not something that happens to you. It's something you create."

2. "Honesty, hard work, and happy habits make a good honey."

3. "Kind actions speak louder than romantic words. But people like the words too."

4. "The three best love actions: attention, listening, working together."

5. "Attention is spending time with as well as focusing on someone."

6. "Listening includes hearing, showing interest in, understanding, and caring."

7. "Working together means you can accomplish, cooperate, and pay your own way."

8. "Notice people who think like you do and who enjoy what you do. Talk to them to see if you might want to spend more time with them."

9. "Good character lasts longer than good looks."

10. "Genuine affirmation and good manners are the best charm."

11. Go on a date together and practice.

CHAPTER 8

My Teen Is Under So Much Pressure

So reinforce your teen to manage it.

"I have no life. All I have is homework and more homework."

"My dad insists that I be the best on the volleyball team. It's not enough that I make high grades, give my best at church, and work as a team player. I have to be the best at everything."

Most of the pressures your teens face come from sources outside your home: school, homework, sports, work, church, and demands by both caring and not-so-caring friends. But some pressures parents add, either deliberately or by accident. You think you're motivating your teen to do *his* best, but you're actually coercing him to be *the* best and communicating that if he does not reach that standard, you'll reject him. It can be tough to tell the difference between healthy pressures that motivate and harsh pressures that immobilize. So invite God's timeless wisdom to show you how to sort healthy pressures from destructive ones and how to equip your teen to manage both.

When you or another parent expect your teen to juggle extraordinary pressures, demanding excellence in school, sports, and spirituality, you usually mean well. You want to motivate. But too much pressure makes adolescents feel powerless and worthless.

Taking away pressures won't fix this. You may be a parent who expects too little from your teen. You cover for her mistakes. You excuse poor school performance with, "That teacher was too hard." You excuse ugly attitudes with, "Things have been tough for her lately." You excuse laziness with, "She has so much going that there's no way she can keep a job or help with chores at home. I can just give her what she needs." You excuse lack of involvement at church with, "She doesn't like organized religion." These motivated teens feel just as powerless and worthless.

The solution is of course to balance pressures, to present expectations and resources that enable your teen to juggle well an adult load of responsibilities. As teens practice at home in the presence of your tutelage, they become able to honor God in all areas of life. They learn how to manage school, part-time work, home responsibilities, church service, and well-maintained relationships. As a parent you can modify the pressures you place, show your teen what outside pressures to drop and keep, and help your teen turn from carbon to diamonds as she or he balances pressures.

Goal—This chapter guides parents to see reasonable pressure as a creative force and to equip their teens to take on the right amount and the right kind of pressure. Then whether the pressures are creative or destructive, parents will equip their teens to respond in God's way to each one.

PARENT WORKSHOP

Draw from these ideas to lead a one-hour parent workshop.

1. Notice What Pressure Does

You'll need a stack of cards, an instruction poster, and for each parent a mini-handout. Prepare and post the instruction poster or display instructions on a computer-generated projection. Duplicate the handout, about four to a page, and cut apart. Arrange the chairs in groups of five. If you expect fewer than ten parents, arrange chairs in one group.

As parents enter, gather them in teams of about five (the odd number helps parents without a spouse not feel like a fifth wheel). Then start another team of five when that one fills up. Instruct teams to start as soon as they arrive on the instructions you have posted, which say:

Tell your group the weather report in your life including:

- Current conditions
- A seven-day forecast
- The barometric pressure (Low pressure indicates cloudy weather; rising pressure means clear weather is on its way.)

- One silver lining in any clouds over your head
- No whining, only positive comments about the good or the challenge that weather presents to you

After all parents have arrived and most or all have shared, point out:

During this session we'll be talking about pressures our teens face and what we parents can do about those pressures. We often think of pressure as negative. Weather illustrates that there are some good pressure. High barometric pressure means sunny weather.

Invite parents to tell about a pressure they've faced that has brought sunny results, such as a deadline at work that prompted them to get the project completed.

After several parents share, explain:

More pressure doesn't directly mean more good weather. Too much pressure can immobilize. In this session our goal is to find ways to use good pressure as it's meant to be used and to minimize negative pressure.

Give each parent a copy of this mini-handout. Ask parents to use one of the three types of pressure as an object lesson to describe the way they believe God wants them to parent their teens through pressure:

A vise is an example of good pressure because it holds two boards together until they can become a self-standing piece of furniture. Too much vise pressure could damage the wood. Or a vise placed in the wrong place, such as on human fingers, could cause harm. But when used as intended, vises help wood move to accomplish a higher purpose.

A pressure cooker needs heat to work. It needs just enough heat for just the right time to create the pressure that produces tender and tasty foods. The heat produces the pressure that cooks the food. Without the heat the food won't cook. Without a consistent amount of pressure, the food won't cook well. But when the heat or the pressure get too high, both the pressure cooker and the food inside explode.

A barometer measures changes in air pressure. When the air pressure changes, the weather changes along with it. Interestingly, low pressure indicates cloudy weather, and high pressure indicates clear weather. Parents can exert just enough pressure to create clear weather for teenagers.

Because a pressure cooker is sealed, no one can see the pressure or watch how well the food is cooking. Users must depend on a pressure indicator valve that tells them how much pressure is building and how fast. Similarly, we can't feel air pressure; we have to watch the barometer to see the coming weather. With a vise we have to get clues from tightness of the two wood pieces about how much pressure is enough.

- What pressure indicator valves show our teenagers are experiencing too much pressure?

  Samples:
    - *Trouble concentrating*
    - *Temper gets worse*
    - *Tolerance gets less*
    - *Argue more*
    - *Cry over little things that don't usually upset your teen*
    - *Fall asleep*
    - *Crumble at the least challenge*
    - *Display more anger*

- You can let pressure out of a pressure cooker by adjusting the heat under it or by venting it. What adjustments have helped your teenager vent or reduce some of the pressure?

  Samples:
    - *Take a nap*
    - *Allow some time to cool down*
    - *Give step-by-step help to do the big project*
    - *Sit next to a teen while he works on a tough school subject*
    - *Do homework early in afternoon or evening rather than late at night*
    - *Get plenty of sleep the night before*
    - *Follow steady rules that allow no ugly talk*
    - *Insist that he keep a closed mouth rather than say something he'll regret*

- What readings show the pressure is producing good "food"?

  Samples:
    - *Joy*
    - *Accomplishment*
    - *Good pride in those accomplishments*

- *Solving problems*
- *Feelings of belonging*
- *Triumph*
- *Finishing duties with time to spare*
- *Refreshment after good hard work*

- **What readings, similar to a barometer, will help us know what's coming with our teenagers?**
  Samples:
  - *When something exciting is happening every night, your teen will likely experience a meltdown emotionally by the fifth or sixth night.*
  - *When teens return from a mission trip or a lock-in at church, they will be so physically exhausted that they will question their spiritual growth. (HINT: Elijah had the same problem in 1 Kings 18–19, and God's prescription was to sleep and eat good food until he recovered.)*
  - *After they invest in homework regularly, they will tend to do well on a test.*
  - *When they go to Sunday morning Bible study and worship regularly, they tend to feel a part of things at church.*

- **What vises seem to hold our teens together?**
  Samples:
  - *Knowing the test is coming makes our teens study.*
  - *Knowing the friend will call makes our teen get chores done so she can talk without having to stop.*
  - *Parental rules of letting you know where they'll be and who chaperones keeps them making good party choices.*
  - *Having to call after school to say they are safely home lets teens know someone cares about the details of their day.*

2. Bolster the Supports

You'll need Bibles, hymnals or another set of hardback books, and a box of flat toothpicks—the ones that break the most easily. Separate the toothpicks into sets of ten, a set for each parent expected, and place the sets across a table or another convenient place. Consider choosing a room with carpet to help the toothpicks stand up.

Give each parent ten toothpicks and a hymnal. Challenge them:
Balance your hymnbook on the toothpick and then add pressure to the top of the hymnal.

Discreetly jot down parents' reactions when the toothpicks break, and after asking what happened to the toothpick, read parents' reactions.

We can think of the toothpicks as our teenagers and the books as the pressures on their backs. Rather than let them break, we can add more support to their lives so they can hold up the hymnals. Even with large pressures, no matter how small our teen feels, and no matter how weak you as a parent feel, God will show you several places to find support and energies.

Direct all parents to start again, this time adding more toothpicks to support the hymnal, letting each represent an element of support in Romans 12:9–21. Allow them to add other examples of support, but let at least half their toothpicks represent one of these Romans 12 actions. In so doing parents will choose five actions from the passage. The other toothpicks can represent other biblical actions such as family or good friends or making the most of every hour (Deut. 6:4–9; Eph. 6:4; Prov. 17:17; Eph. 5:15–17). Parents may, but don't have to, cite a particular passage for those.

Examples:
- *Do what is right so guilt and regret won't also burden you (Rom. 12:17).*
- *Share Bible promises or invite your teen to cite one.*
- *Teens love their family sincerely, and parents love their teen sincerely with affection, attention, and steady guidance (Rom. 12:9).*
- *Show your teen how to manage the pressure (Deut. 6:4–9).*
- *Show devotion by helping each other with projects and stresses (Rom. 12:10).*
- *Raise teens in relationship to and according to the instruction of God (Eph. 6:4).*
- *Call on God for energy (zeal/fervor) (Rom. 12:11).*
- *Develop and maintain healthy friendships (Prov. 17:17).*
- *Courageously say no even when it's rough.*
- *Choose patience, recognizing patience is not a feeling but a deliberate choice (Rom. 12:12).*
- *Insist your teen get a nap or other physical rest.*
- *Notice when your teen needs a boost of encouragement and provide it with a glass of water, a back rub, or a "you can do it" cheer (Rom. 12:13).*

- *Make the most of the time you have (Eph. 5:15–17).*
- *Show your teen how to call on God's power to live in harmony with your family, doing what is right and kind no matter how tired, how stressed or how pressured they are (Rom. 12:16).*
- *Find time regularly to converse with your teens, at least daily after school and at supper.*
- *Guide your teen to manage rough teachers with the heap-burning-coals philosophy—doing the right thing back no matter how they are treated (Rom. 12:20).*
- *Provide good books and magazines to read during down time.*
- *"Do not be overcome by evil, but overcome evil with good" (Rom. 12:21).*
- *Double up on what needs doing such as studying in the car while parents are driving to church.*
- *Remember that every action is God's action, not just what happens at church or during church functions.*

While parents keep their hymnbooks on the toothpicks, discuss:
- **How many toothpicks did it take to hold up the hymnal?**
- **Which of the Romans 12 actions help you personally with your pressures and stresses?**
- **Which of the Romans 12 actions might help your teen with his or her pressures and stresses?**

After each question, equalize talking by prompting each parent to give one answer before any parent gives a second one.

Encourage parents to ask their teens which Romans 12 actions would help the most during stresses and what they would like their parents to do to help during stress. Highlight humorously that if a teen says, "Don't make me help with chores this week," or, "Let me be hard to live with," help them know how to get those chores and good attitudes done. But if they ask, "Can I trade dishes with you tonight so I can finish this paper?" offer give-and-take.

 ## Adaptation for a Youth-Parent Meeting

If youth are present, let them answer these questions about how parents can help with stresses, perhaps serving as a panel. Be certain to warn teens ahead of time that they will be asked these questions, so they can think about their responses in advance. Warn them against any kind of parent-attack mode, and encourage a we-can-do-this-together approach.

Pray that God will help parents and teens know how to be family during high pressure times and during everyday stresses. Pray that God will especially guide parents to know how much to expect during stress.

Direct each parent to choose one toothpick with which to mark Romans 12 in their Bibles, while leaving the others to support the hymnals for the next step.

Teaching Tip

Why bother with the toothpicks and the hymnals? Can't you just talk about pressures and supports? If your parents work in construction or architecture, they'll understand supports more immediately. But not all parents work in those fields. Even for those who do, a picture is worth more than a thousand words. So let the many-little-supports-add-up-to-one-big-support picture show that parents' daily guidance of their teens is more powerful than a pep talk before the big test. Similarly, little cuts can destroy a foundation even when we don't notice.

3. Select Pressures Carefully

You'll need the hymnbooks still on toothpicks from step 2, a set of recipe cards or any lined three-by-five-inch cards, and Bibles.

Can you still break the toothpicks, even though there are many of them to support the hymnbook?

As parents try, invite them to share aloud their strategies.

Samples:
- *Push really hard.*
- *Push at an angle.*
- *Find the weak toothpick and push hardest there.*

Agree that sometimes teens do feel like someone is pressing on their backs. Other times they feel poked like this book might feel if it were skin.

Say: **The right amount of pressure can break any support system. Because there are only so many hours in a day and our teens do need to sleep and rest, we must help them choose their commitments.**

Give each parent a recipe card and pen. Direct them to write a recipe for choosing and balancing the commitments, stresses, and pressures of life.

Post these directives on a poster or computer-generated image:

Write a recipe for a balanced teenage life or a recipe that evaluates whether a commitment is a good one to make.

- In your recipe include at least three ingredients.
- Include a phrase from Romans 12:9–21 or another of your favorite Bible passages.
- Include mixing instructions.
- Include cooking/baking instructions.
- Options: acceptable substitutions, how you can tell when it's done, serving instructions, the number it feeds, recommended order of ingredients, what to serve it with.

Two sample recipes:

Blend: Is-this-for-school? Does-this-help-my-teen-become-wiser? And do-we-realistically-have-time-for-this? in a large mixing bowl. Be sure to mash out all lumps of but-everyone-else-is-doing-this and but-I-really-want-this with your there-is-simply-no-more-hours-in-your-day spoon. Pour into a well-rested teen prepared with an enforced bedtime. Bake at ten hours a day for schoolwork and homework. Ice with a nice blend of time with friends and a dash of hobby. Be sure not to put in more than one hobby at a time because it will take away the sweetness. Mix with sincere love and devotion to God in each pursuit. Serve a daily portion along with daily bread.

Combine:
1 Regular school attendance and homework completion
1 Outside school sport/lesson/hobby
1 Regular service opportunity such as sorting clothes at the thrift shop
1 Regular Sunday and Wednesday church attendance
1 Adequate rest plus at least one full afternoon a week to spend just being (Sunday afternoon recommended)
Blend with a good book or magazine every night before bed, a good laugh over supper, and a happy send-off following breakfast for a teen who can do it all. Stir in love, joy, peace, patience, kindness, goodness, gentleness, faithfulness, and self-control. In the case of high-pressure school years, consider choosing a low demand sport/lesson/hobby.

Call for each adult to present his or her recipe. Highlight something wise in each. Suggest that all adults take notes on the back of their recipe cards of insights and ingredients they want to use in helping their teens to "bake their lives" just right.

4. Evaluate the Pressures You Add

You'll need Bibles, and three pages for each team—one marked SCHOOL, one marked CHURCH, and one marked OTHER. Arrange for a timer (perhaps on your wristwatch) and a three-legged stool (or draw an illustration of one.

Say: **Our goal as parents is to let our pressure be motivating and not debilitating. Let's explore how to do this.**

Distribute three pages to each team, one marked SCHOOL, one marked CHURCH, and one marked OTHER. Give them exactly two minutes to fill each with pressures their teen or a teen they know faces. Challenge them to list more than any other team.

Call time at exactly two minutes and lightly fuss that all are to raise their pens and write no more. If you see any parents continuing to write, tease them, that just like teenagers, we try to fit one more item on our list and one more thing into our lives.

Gather all the papers at random on top of a three-legged stool, or on top of a drawing of a three-legged stool. Suggest:

Say: **As we help our teens with pressures, they need three legs:**

1. **Encouragement and motivation. Knowing their families are behind them is the biggest factor of success in school, in pursuing dreams, in sports, in developing talent, and in living for Christ in all these areas.**

2. **Skill training. Our teens need to know how to manage their time so they can get done what they need to do. For example, a teen who has three assignments will fare best if she does the hardest first and ends with the easiest. Then as she gets weary, she can still do good work. Sometimes this reverses if one of the assignments is a takes-as-much-time-as-is-left kind of assignment.**

3. **Choice making. Teens have certain demands already in place; school is their job, and church is their inspiration. But even within those are choices: What classes do I take and at what levels? What ministries do I choose and with how much time commitment? Finding out just what**

God wants your teen to do with each year is the key. And of course God
is just as interested in how your teen learns at school as how your teen
worships at church.

According to the support strategies we listed, the recipes we wrote, and
the three-legged stool philosophy, how does God want you personally as a
parent to act in response to one of the pressures your teen faces? Each of
you tell me one sentence of commitment. (Example: I've been pressing for
all honors classes when I really should press for one honors class.)

Guide the process so it avoids the extremes of "I've been a horrible parent" self-deprecation or sharing horror stories about how bad my teens
make things. Instead encourage a tone of let's-move-on-from-here-to-do-
the-helpful-thing. Insist that every parent contribute at least one comment,
explaining that it can be general and without details.

Supplement as needed with comments from the introduction to this session such as:

Notice whether you've been giving too much or too little pressure, and
adjust accordingly. Work for your teen's best, not *the* best.

5. A Few Tough Ones

*You'll need copies of the scenarios so each parent can have one. Tape to the
wall some specific strategies drawn from earlier steps such as the examples
above and those in this step.*

In real life things don't work quite as smoothly as we wish they did.
On the same day your teen has decided to finish his term paper, he may
come down with the flu. Or another teacher may schedule a test. Let's
discuss together what God might want us to do in these real-life
scenarios.

Urge at least five actions for each.

Your teen wants to go to a Christian college. The tuition for those
schools is so high that your teen will need scholarships. You know that the
cutoff to be considered for those scholarships is a 3.75 grade point aver-
age and a strong score on the ACT or SAT test. The whole time you're
encouraging "learning is more important than grades," you know that college officials will be looking at those grades. How do you work toward
these goals without creating paralyzing pressures for your student?

Your teen is passionate about church. Every time the door is open, your teen is there. He loves the Bible studies, the mission trips, the youth council, the fellowship, the work with senior citizens Saturdays, the share times, and more. The problem is that he's at church so often he doesn't get his homework done. He says homework is second to church because the spiritual is primary. You know the spiritual is basic to every aspect of life (Col. 3:23). How do you guide your teen to balance his life in honor of God?

Your teen has too few pressures. In an effort to simplify her life, she has dropped back to easier classes in school, fewer hours at work, and only goes to church on Sunday mornings. She doesn't even go out much on weekends. She just stays at home and watches television or plays computer games. When you try to prod her to do more, she says the stress is not worth it. You know she needs more motivation for several reasons: She's not using her gifts; she's not building relationships; she's afraid to try new things; she's quite simply bored in all areas of her life. How do you light a fire under her in ways that don't put her down but definitely speed her up? (HINT: See the principles in chapter 1.)

You admit it. You have expected too much from your teen. You want your teen to be the best in sports, the top in his class, and a leader at church. You're backing off, but now that you do, you notice that your teen continues to expect too much from himself. He won't cut himself any slack and goes to bed way too late every night after practicing and studying relentlessly. How can you help your teen lighten up without making your teen believe he can't do it or that you don't care what he does? How can you prod godly balance?

To help with discussion refer parents to the toothpick strategies, recipes for balance, and three-legged stool.

Time Note

If you have extra time, put these questions in a paper sack and direct parents to take turns drawing one out and answering it:

- What is the source of your teens' most severe pressures? Friends? Teachers? Family? Self?

- What is the difference between healthy stress and dangerous stress, and how do you balance these?
- Pressure can set teens up for traps like cheating, bragging, and lying. How do you equip your teen to avoid these at all cost?
- What's dangerous about assuming teens (or you) can do one more thing if they just want to, or if they just call upon God's power?
- What is the best way to manage pressure from friends?
- What is the best way to manage pressure from teachers?
- What is the best way to manage pressure from family?
- What is the best way to manage pressure from self?

Adaptation for a Youth-Parent Meeting

If youth are present, enlist each one of them to write a story about pressure, their own or the pressures of someone they know. Then use them in place of the step 5 examples. Be certain to verify ahead of time that youth don't mind your using the personal example in the workshop, letting them read the changed-for-privacy version.

The Point

Make a copy of "The Point" on colored paper, perhaps screened with a pressure cooker, to give to parents.

Similar to a pressure cooker that must be vented and given just the right amount of heat, our teens need enough pressure to produce a tasty life, but not enough to cause them to explode. Work hand-in-hand with God to adjust the heat and vent the steam while you enjoy a good life with your teenager.

Give each parent a copy of "The Point" printed on a sketch of a pressure cooker.

Pray God's guidance in our own and our teens' pressures.

➤ The Point

Show your teen how to call on God's supernatural power to do what is right and good no matter how tired, how stressed, or how pressured he may be. Stress is never an excuse for acting ugly.

"*Be careful to do what is right. . . . Do not be overcome by evil, but overcome evil with good*" (Rom. 12:17, 21).

Because good pressure can create diamonds, show your teen how to harvest motivation, accomplishment, and other benefits from even the harshest pressures. As your teen deliberately chooses to honor others and complete tasks, she will not just endure the pressure but will sparkle.

HOME DISCUSSION GUIDE

Send this page home with parents, mailing to any who were not able to attend, or mail to each parent a few days after the session as a follow-up prompter to practice "The Point."

"The Point" of our last parent meeting was to show your teen how to find power to do what is right and good no matter how tired, how stressed, or how pressured he is.

This point is based on the fact that no matter how severe our pressures, we can find a way to manage. Sometimes this means dropping something, and sometimes this means bearing up under it until we can drop something. And no matter how painful the pressures are for you or your teenager, "Be careful to do what is right. . . . Do not be overcome by evil, but overcome evil with good" (Rom. 12:17, 21).

Because good pressure can create diamonds, show your teen how to harvest motivation, accomplishment, and other benefits from even the harshest pressures. As your teen deliberately chooses to honor others and complete tasks, she will not just endure the pressure but will sparkle. Because continuing pressure can crush those diamonds, help your teen detour past relentless pressure.

Together with your teenager create a pressure survival kit. Go through your house and find items that could be used in times of pressure. Be silly as well as serious. Each of you might want to pick about three items in a specified time and then bring them back to the kitchen table to share. Some examples:

- Two aspirin tablets to show, "I won't turn to drugs no matter how great the pressure, with the exception of occasional aspirin for headaches."
- Scissors to show, "Cutting something from my schedule is a sign of strength and focus, not a sign of weakness."
- A calendar to show, "Every semester I'll evaluate what's coming up, and I'll cut out what I absolutely cannot do, even if I want to do it very much. Then a month into the semester, I'll add it back in if I can."
- A pillow to show, "I will treasure good rest and protect it so I have the energy I need to manage everything I'm doing."
- A pair of glasses or sunglasses to show, "I may need a parent to watch over me to make certain I don't commit to too much or try to put things in the wrong priority. I'll also ask them to make certain I don't drop too much."
- An ad in the newspaper to show, "Just because something looks good in the pictures or on the surface doesn't mean it's for me."
- A rubber band to show, "We are flexible in our house. If one night is highly pressured, we'll take it easy the next night."
- The same rubber band to show, "We are held together, and we'll each stretch to help the other."

Keep the discussion lighthearted but supportive. Assure your teenagers: I am here to support you and to show you ways to handle the pressures of life. God will guide us. Together we can do it. That's what family is for.

NEWSLETTER IDEA

Use these as a base for a parent newsletter, for youth-written articles, or for the parent section of the church newsletter.

What Are Characteristics of a Healthy Parent?
(Thanks to Phil Briggs & Friends)

Parents are like the gatekeepers. They decide how much pressure will hit their teens and how many resources their teen will find to stay standing when the floods of pressure come through. Good parents display these characteristics:

- Enjoy their teens
- Have confidence in their right and responsibility to parent
- Set and maintain reasonable expectations
- Courageously help their teens say no to certain pressures and yes to other pressures
- Spend time with each other and with their teens
- Deliberately impart skills to their teens (e.g., people skills, money management, problem-solving, temptation-resisting)
- Set clear rules and show how to follow them. Then they enforce those rules.
- Show teens how to honor God in all areas of life, not just church
- Communicate well
- Equip for the strains of adolescence
- Give enough pressure to create a diamond but not so much pressure that the diamond shatters

These characteristics are choices, not something parents are born with. You can choose each of these with God's power and guidance each and every day.

E-MAIL IDEAS

Choose from these parent support ideas, tips, and strategies especially for electronic transmission. (Remember: Don't create an E-mail Elite; print out and mail the messages to any parents who don't have E-mail).

As you evaluate how God wants you to help your teens with their pressures, pray these questions and invite God's insights:

- God, am I more the one who helps my teen face pressure or the one who adds the pressure? How do you want me to change?
- God, am I more likely to give too little pressure or too much pressure to my teen? Which direction should I move?
- God, if I were the floodgate, how wide would you want me to open the pressure flood for each of my teens and why?
- While pondering specific pressures, invite God to show you the answers to these questions:
  1. Can it be dropped?
  2. Does it need to stay?
  3. Does it need extra encouragement or a new skill?
  4. How can it be done with good balance?
  5. What time of the day does God want my teen to accomplish this?

And if you're sending the E-mail to a cell phone, here's a short one: *While showing your teen how to manage pressures, encourage your teen to start with the hard stuff and reward self with the fun stuff.*

WHAT TEENAGERS WANT PARENTS TO KNOW

Choose from these questions that invite your teens to share with you anonymous quotes, quips, and comments via E-mail or anonymous survey. Feel free to choose one question at a time as the "Question of the Week."

I'll combine your ideas with no names or identifying details to distribute to parents. Feel free to answer a question that's not here or to suggest another question for everyone to answer:

- How have your parents equipped you to manage stress and pressure?
- When have your parents added to the pressures with expectations you could never meet? With expectations that were reasonable?
- When have your parents helped you take away a destructive pressure?

- What factors in your family make your stress easier? Harder?
- Your parents have stress too. What do you admire about the way they manage it?
- Why do you think so many teenagers feel so much pressure?
- What actions would God suggest for managing your current stress?

TROUBLESHOOTING

Suggest these actions to implement when a teen does not display the expected behavior.

Suppose your teen has way too much going. Try these actions:
- Sit down and decide what can go, or what can be streamlined.
- Calendar what needs to be done so teens know how much to do each day. For example: For the research paper, get the note cards done by Tuesday, the rough draft by Thursday, and the final draft by Saturday.
- Set up a reward system that helps teens get everything done. For example, all homework must be done before Wednesday night church or before going out on Saturday nights. Then, because they want to get to youth group and out with friends, they'll work efficiently and won't have to do homework late after church when they're too tired to concentrate. They can also be rested enough to handle the demands of the rest of the week.

Suppose your teen doesn't have enough going and needs a little pressure. Try these actions:
- Sit down and decide what else your teen needs to be doing, such as taking a more challenging class at school, working part-time, or taking responsibility for another chore at home.
- Explain by what time on what day certain things must happen. Withhold a privilege until those things happen.
- Celebrate successful completion of each milestone.

Bonus Idea

This idea is a haven magnet. Guide parents to display it as a reminder to create a happy home.

Possible way to use: Duplicate this house on heavy paper. Back with magnetic tape so it becomes a magnet for the refrigerator or filing cabinet.

Haven Magnet

TO
MAKE A
HAVEN, LET EVERY
MEMBER HAVE A CHANCE TO
TELL THE STORIES OF
THE DAY. THEN EACH
ONE CHERISH THE
STORY, OFFER SUPPORT,
ADVICE, HUGS AS
NEEDED, AND TRULY
BE AN INTERWORKING
BODY OF CARE.

CHAPTER 9

My Teen Didn't Mean to Give in to Temptation

So armor your teen against the destroy-their-lives dangers that lurk everywhere.

"I didn't mean to. I just don't see why I have to be in a wheelchair for life. It's not like I wrecked the car on purpose or anything."

"It was just one time of cheating. I don't see why that should keep me from getting in the top ten. Without that I won't be accepted into the college I want!"

Dangers lurk everywhere, eager to snare your teen. One or two mistakes can mess up a teen's entire life. And even smaller temptations like gossip and slander can destroy friendships God wants your teens to have. A persistent devil, who is hopping mad because he has been thrown to earth, is taking his rage out on Christians who care (Rev. 12:17). And he convinces people that even if they mess up, an "I didn't *mean* to" or a genuine "I'm sorry" will make it all OK. But it doesn't. The legs are still paralyzed. The well-deserved zero remains in the grade book. And the former friends still sting from the barbs of betrayal.

The good news is that your teens are not powerless. They have at their fingertips the power of God Himself and the strategies He demonstrated while living on earth in the person Jesus Christ. The tough part is one little detail that we Christians are prone to forget: The best way to fight temptation is to flee from it.

Goal—This chapter guides parents to show their teens how to flee and how to free themselves from the snares of temptation.

PARENT WORKSHOP

Draw from these ideas to lead a one-hour parent workshop.

1. Name the Temptations

You'll need Bibles, tables covered with paper tablecloths, and markers.

As parents enter, gather them around tables covered with paper tablecloths and direct them to doodle temptations on the paper. Encourage words, doodlings, drawings, descriptions, or a combination. Challenge each table of parents to fill their tables with more temptations than on any other tablecloth. Suggest they include temptations both teenagers and parents face. Refer them to Exodus 20; 1 Corinthians 6:9–11; Galatians 5:19–21; 1 Timothy 6; and other lists of sins in the Bible.

Circulate and suggest "everyday" temptations as well as the biggies such as stealing, murder, adultery, and more.

Suppose you were one of the devil's assistants. What especially sneaky temptation would you present to Christians, an area where they may not be paying enough attention to resist?

The competition will challenge parents to move past the classics and into more sneaky and subtle temptations.

Examples of all kinds of temptations:
- *Gossip*
- *Cruel talk*
- *Slander*
- *Discord*
- *Adultery*
- *Stealing*
- *Cheating (a form of stealing)*
- *Deceit*
- *Arrogance*
- *Greed*
- *Keeping self at center of attention (There is a God, and you are not Him.)*
- *Swindling*

- *Bragging in a way that makes others feel like losers*
- *Going too far sexually*
- *Lust*
- *Using people physically*
- *Using people financially*
- *Using people emotionally*
- *Using people spiritually, or in any way*
- *Giving up*
- *Driving too fast (endangers you and your passengers)*
- *Drinking alcohol under 18*
- *Running stoplights*
- *Breaking any traffic law*
- *Criticism*
- *Idolatry*
- *Clothes worship*
- *Materialism*
- *Cussing*
- *Misusing God's name*
- *Working and never taking a rest*
- *Dishonoring parents*
- *Murder*
- *Lying*
- *Not telling the whole truth*
- *Coveting*
- *Envy*
- *Impurity*
- *Hatred*
- *Jealousy*
- *Fits of rage*
- *Selfish ambition*
- *Factions*
- *Drunkenness*
- *Gluttony*
- *Hurting your own body*
- *Hurting someone else's body*
- *Refusing to cherish family*

- *Exasperating children*
- *Holier-than-thou-ness*

As tables of parents report what they have doodled, point out:

You have shown that Satan doesn't come to us in a red suit with a pitchfork. If he did, we would notice him. Instead he comes in ways that subtly but insidiously cause us to hurt people (including ourselves) in ways we never would do on purpose.

The best way to fight temptation is to flee from it. We tend to flirt with temptation instead, to claim that because of Christ we are strong enough to resist. Then we, and our teens, get into situations where we are ripe for temptation. Because the devil is so crafty, he gets us before we know it. We *can* resist; it's just that we tend not to when a delicious situation presents itself. For teens this might be a romantic moment with the one they deeply adore. It's not that they mean to go too far physically. It's that they don't want to spoil the romantic moment. Or it might be driving the car a little too fast because they're late for school. They didn't mean to kill the pedestrian or to create a baby. But the coming baby and the family of the pedestrian suffer just as definitely.

We as parents cannot leave our teens to the devil's schemes. He's stronger than they are. So we must provide the chaperoning, the training, the supervision, and the strategies that show our teens how to resist in ways that keep them looking cool. Jesus offered profound strategies in Matthew 4. In other passages Jesus demonstrated the power of surrounding Himself with caring people and staying away from dangerous situations. Even He didn't go into Jerusalem before a certain time.

Invite parents to name examples of accidental sins that have caused huge sadness:

Sample:
- *One night of romance led to a pregnancy.*
- *Lying destroyed trust between a teen and parents.*
- *Sneaking out to see someone you liked led to that person hurting you, and you had no one to call for help.*
- *Yelling in anger caused someone to say something horrible, and those words haunted the hearer for months.*

During this session we'll explore many temptation-resisting strategies, the most powerful one being to flee. Another solution to the temptation

problem is to do the right thing on purpose so we don't do the wrong thing by accident. And a third is to decide ahead of time what we will and won't do—through vows and through recognizing what matters.

Adaptation For a Youth-Parent Meeting

If youth are present, they will love this doodling process. Suggest that they think of temptations people of all ages face and to participate in the reporting of and the naming of how Satan appears.

2. Notice the Devil's Tricks

You'll need Bibles, markers, masking tape circles, and construction paper. Place on each table a stack of construction paper.

To resist temptation we must first discover how the devil tempts. Open your Bible to Matthew 4:1–10 to find the strategies the devil used to tempt Jesus. And by the way, because Jesus was tempted severely but never sinned, we know that temptation is not a sin. Giving in is the sin.

Give teams about two minutes to write the strategies, one to a page, and tape them to the wall.

Include:
- *Came at Jesus when He was weak.*
- *Hit Jesus where He was weak—hunger*
- *Taunted Him with, "If you really are . . ."*
- *Jesus threw resisting strategies right back at Him: When Jesus quoted Scripture, the devil quoted Scripture too.*
- *Twisted the truth; didn't use the Scripture as it was meant to be used*
- *Offered power*
- *Had a condition for every gift*

Tape these to the wall with tape circles you have prepared.
What other ways has the devil tempted you or a Bible time person?
Add these ideas to the wall.
Samples might include:
- *Pretending to be your friend*
- *Making wrong look right*
- *Telling only half truths*
- *Convinces you this is just a little sin and doesn't matter*

Each of you pick one of the temptations doodled on your table and write a letter to a Christian teen to get him or her to do this. Write from the devil's viewpoint, using one of his strategies.

Circulate and encourage parents to be especially sneaky, making that wrong action look not so bad at all or at least excusable under the circumstances. Prompt team members to help one another with their letters, repeating that as we write these letters we'll better understand the temptations our teens face.

As letters are complete, take them up and shuffle them. Explain:

In the next step we'll exchange letters and resist these temptations. But first we need to find some biblical ways to do this.

3. Notice Jesus' Resisting Strategies

You'll need Bibles and construction paper. Resupply construction paper if teams are running low.

Again search Matthew 4:1–10, this time seeking Jesus' resistance strategies. Make posters to hang on the wall, with one resistance strategy per page, just as we did before. This time look in other Bible passages for more Bible strategies for resisting temptation such as in your own favorite passages.

Circulate and supply passages such as Romans 12:1–2; 1 Corinthians 6:18; 10:13–14; 1 Timothy 6:11; 2 Timothy 2:22 to those who want them.

Sample resisting strategies might include:
- *Jesus countered the devil with Scripture.*
- *Jesus saw the half truths.*
- *Jesus saw the misapplied truth and supplied a correct one.*
- *Jesus told Satan to go away.*
- *Jesus did not eat even though He was very hungry.*
- *We can be doing the right thing so we have no time for bad things (Rom. 12:1–2).*
- *Flee and pursue right instead (2 Tim. 2:22).*

Redistribute the shuffled temptation letters and challenge parents, confirming that no one has the letter he or she wrote:

Now write a letter back to the "devil," resisting the letter with one or more of the resisting strategies we found in Scripture and are now posted on the wall.

Circulate and encourage parents as they write, urging them to be specific and to speak from the viewpoint of a teenager.

Call for volunteers to read the letters in their hands from the devil followed by the letter they wrote that resists this temptation. Highlight a wise insight in each, including a way the temptation was powerful and a way the resisting strategy was more powerful.

What new nuance about resisting or tempting did you discover during this process?

Say: **There is no way to anticipate all the temptations you or your teen might face. But thinking through examples as we have done prepares us with strategies. Because we resist some of the devil's schemes, we can manage others. How might you do this same exercise at home with your teenagers?**

Samples:

- *Parent and teen each write a letter and trade for the other to resist.*
- *Have a back-and-forth sparring in which one of you pretends to be the devil who presents a reason to do a wrong and then the other resists it, and then the "devil" gives another reason to do it, followed by resisting, followed by tempting, and so on.*

As parents share ideas, suggest that they note on the paper tablecloth ideas and strategies they want to remember. Then let them tear off that section of the tablecloth and use it to mark Matthew 4 in their Bibles (leaving the section of the tablecloth that has all the doodles).

4. Memory Formula

You'll need Bibles and photocopies of the Bonus Idea.

We've discovered several strategies and applied them to several situations. In addition to transferring this inside information to our teenagers, we need to know how we parents can armor our teens against temptation.

We'll overview four basic equipping actions that form a puzzle in our Bonus section. Give each parent two copies of this Bonus and let them solve the puzzle. Encourage them to keep the extra copy for their teenagers to enjoy solving.

When all finish the puzzle, explain:

The first armor is *glee*. God wants our teens to be so busy doing the right thing that they don't have time to do the wrong thing. If you have substance-free parties at your house that are absolutely fun, there won't be as much temptation to go to parties with alcohol or drugs. This strategy is based on Romans 12:1–2 and 2 Timothy 2:22.

Invite parents to jot up and down on the paper tablecloth the first name of each of their teens and then for each letter name a fun thing they could guide that teen to do to prevent some of the temptations doodled there.

The second action is *flee* (based on 1 Cor. 6:18; 1 Cor. 10:14; 1 Tim. 6:11). For example: Institute a rule that your teens flee by going to no parties where alcohol or other drugs of any kind are served. If they don't know of alcohol until they get there, a good strategy for your nondrivers is to drop them at the party and then to park up the block. Your teen goes into the party and checks things out. If she sees anything suspicious, she just casually leaves and walks to your car without a scene. Drivers can walk to their own car. What if your teen says she can witness to those at the party and that she won't drink?

Discuss the fact that most parties with alcohol or substances are centered around getting high. The presence of a nondrinker does little if anything to change that. Encourage parents to share other ideas for helping youth flee temptation.

Samples:

- *Parent knows name and phone number of adult chaperone of all parties.*
- *Parent is always in the house when parties go on or when the opposite sex is over.*
- *Only one rider is allowed in car at all times.*

We can also prevent temptation by noticing how *free* we stay without it (John 8:36; 10:10). Guide your teens in a process of unshackling themselves by reminding them of the freedom they have by not doing a certain wrong. Do this as a game.

Guide parents to play the game.

Examples:

- *By not drinking, I'm free to remember the party.*
- *By not lying, I'm free not to have to cover up my lies.*
- *By not having sex, I am free not to worry when my period is late.*
- *By not having sex, I'm free not to have to explain to my spouse why I slept with someone else.*
- *By not cheating, I'm free to know that I'll never get caught.*
- *By treating everyone as someone of value, people are free to trust me.*
- *By enjoying my days, I'm free from the pressure of feeling I must have an opposite-sex relationship.*

Say: **The next action is fret.** *Fret* **is our way to say, "Worry the biblical way." By looking ahead to bad things that could happen (and usually do) if you choose to do wrong, you can choose to do right. In this way the devil doesn't catch you off guard. One good way is to guide our teens to write and keep vows. Let them search the Bible and find just what God wants them to do when. Show them passages to start them on their way and help them compose the vows.**

Guide parents to compose on the tablecloths a vow a teen could take on one of these topics: gossip, lying, cheating, alcohol and drug use, parties, cheating, or another topic of parents' choosing. Here are samples for alcohol, sexual purity, and parties:

> Because specific people in both the Old and New Testament took a vow to drink no alcohol (Dan. 1:8; Luke 1:15) and because alcohol does me no good, I vow from this day forward to drink no alcohol. I will depend on God for strength not to do so (Phil. 4:13).
>
> _____(signature)
>
> _____(date)
>
> As a commitment to the spouse I will one day choose, the children I will one day bear or adopt, and to myself, I choose to have no sex until the day I marry. This will keep me from using people or being used (1 Thess. 4:3–8). It also will equip me for true love.
>
> _____(signature)
>
> _____(date)
>
> Because I want to have true fun, I will attend only parties where people are treasured—no people put-downs, no drugs or alcohol to medicate people into not caring, no sneaking off to bedrooms. I will walk into the party and check it out while my parent (or my car if I am driving) waits a block away. If I see people-using going on, I will casually leave and walk to my car. I also will have plenty of my own parties (Ps. 118:24).
>
> _____(signature)
>
> _____(date)

With permission from each who wrote one, duplicate these vows for all parents to use in their families. You can duplicate selected ones if some would rather not duplicate theirs.

How does deciding ahead of time what you will and won't do fight temptation? Would it be possible to take too many vows?

 **Teaching Tip**

Why bother solving the puzzle with four temptation-fighting strategies? Why not just tell parents what to do? Because working with the words helps parents remember the principles and how to do them. What goes in one ear tends to go out the other if there is not some activity that uses that information.

5. My Support System

You'll need Bibles, white poster board cut into credit-card-sized pieces, and markers/pens that write on poster board without smearing.

Vows are a critical strength builder, but they are not enough. We all need support systems to outsmart temptation. We can be that for our teens by letting them draw on our strength. To do this we'll have to establish rules and enforce them; we'll also have to provide supervision. This gives our teens a living laboratory of how to choose the right things when they have enough of their own strength to do so.

Challenge parents to name for each vow a set of three household rules or parental actions that would help a teen keep that vow. *For the party vow, the three might be:*

- I'll know what house you're going to and who chaperones. You can always have an alternate party at our house.
- I'll wait up for you to welcome you home and hear about the party. This not only gives your teen someone to tell good news; it also lets them know they'll get caught if they drink or do drugs, so they'll have an anchor to keep them from drifting into it.
- I'll come pick you up *anytime* a party gets crazy, whether with ugly talk, wild behavior, drugs, boredom, or whatever.

After parents share samples of their trios, give them one of the credit-card-sized poster boards and direct them to write on it a vow of action and supervision that equips their teens to manage temptation.

Provide extra credit-card-sized poster board for parents to take home and use with their teenagers as they write vows together.

 Time Note

Steps like 4 and 5 can take longer that planned because there are so many areas to explore. That's OK because once parents begin to talk, they tend to continue talking outside the session. To keep within the time allotted and to make the in-session conversation meaningful, you may have to make some of the responses private and then not take time to report. This allows the learning to be more private, a just-between-God-and-me sort of growth time.

6. The Little Stuff Is Not So Little

You'll need Bibles.

As we *glee, free, flee,* and *fret,* and as we help our teens keep their *vows,* we must avoid a temptation ourselves: to assume that our kids are doing OK or that their temptations are no big deal. Why is temptation always a danger no matter how good our teens are?

Comment from the introduction to explain that one small mistake can change our teens' lives forever. Include also the fact that giving in to little temptations subtly leads to sadness over time. Call for each parent around the table to name a little temptation teens give in to, assuming that sin is no big deal.

Samples:

- *Gossip, because it slanders people God created.*
- *Excusing sin for our convenience. Sample:*
- *"It's OK if we talk about her because we don't really like her anyway."*
- *Rumors, because they cause people to miss the real truth about good people.*
- *Lying, because one lie leads to another.*
- *Snobbery, because everyone is worth speaking to.*
- *Cruel words, even in jest, because all of us need all the help we can get.*

Pray for motivation to be just as vigorous about arming against these "little" temptations as the "big" ones.

Adaptation For a Youth-Parent Meeting

If youth are present, invite them to tell about how "little" sins like aloofness and gossip have hurt them deeply. They might want to write this anonymously to protect both the hurt and the hurter.

The Point

Make a copy of "The Point" on colored paper to give to parents.

As you give parents a copy of "The Point" to take home, challenge parents to keep their teens away from certain settings, and to instill in them a profound commitment to do the right thing at all times so evil has no room to wiggle in.

➤ The Point

Communicate that fleeing is the most effective temptation-resisting strategy. Following close behind is the strategy of deciding ahead of time what you will and won't do. Then work together to learn and practice other strategies.

"No temptation has seized you except what is common to man. And God is faithful; he will not let you be tempted beyond what you can bear. But when you are tempted, he will also provide a way out so that you can stand up under it" (1 Cor. 10:13).

Because temptation is part of every believer's life, we must each learn to resist it rather than use it as an excuse for wrongdoing.

HOME DISCUSSION GUIDE

Send this page home with parents, mailing to any who were not able to attend, or mail it to each parent a few days after the session as a follow-up prompter to practice the point.

The Point of our last parent meeting was to communicate fleeing as the most effective temptation-resisting strategy.

It's not bad to be tempted, but it is bad to give in. Work with your teens to armor them against the life-changing pain that certain behaviors bring, and show them how to flee.

God promises: *"No temptation has seized you except what is common to man. And God is faithful; he will not let you be tempted beyond what you can bear. But when you are tempted, he will also provide a way out so that you can stand up under it"* (1 Cor. 10:13).

Together with your teen find those ways. Explain: "Because the devil is crafty, temptation is part of every believer's life. He gets us just where we hurt and just where we don't expect him to tempt. So we must get away from tempting situations whenever possible. And we must gather an arsenal of resisting strategies for the times we can't get away. In so doing we learn to resist temptation rather than use it as an excuse for wrongdoing."

Name these strategies with a categories game. (One category game is Scattergories® available in toy stores or discount department stores.) Give a card to each of your teens and to yourself for each round. Allow about a minute (or use the timer in your game) to list six in the first category. The first category is Temptations I Face.

Follow with the category: How to Resist Temptation. Samples include:
- Decide ahead of time what I will do and won't do.
- Stay away from certain situations.
- See that temptation is real.
- Take temptation seriously.
- Get around other people who resist too.
- Ask for help.
- Know my weaknesses.
- Expect to be tempted in weaknesses I don't yet know.
- Stubbornly believe that wrong always harms me.

Compare your lists and circle ones unique to you or your teen. Underline ones you both share. Play another round to list another six temptations. Again compare.

Repeat the listing, comparing, and circling for the next categories:
- Times temptation is especially tough to resist
- Resisting strategies I use or could use (This picks from the general lists created earlier.)
- More resisting strategies from Matthew 4:1–10

- How my family can help me resist temptations
- How I want to help you with your temptations

After each listing, compare your lists and circle ones you want to start practicing as a family. During the game and discussion about the game, you can teach resisting strategies, vows, and supervision strategies that you learned during the parent meeting.

Throughout the game communicate that you and your teens walk together on the temptation road, and together you can help each other. Because you are the parent and a little further down the temptation-resisting road, you will provide supervision and a little more help. But over-all, both of you are on the same road.

Together claim the 1 Corinthians 10:13 promise, and pledge to practice it rather than just assume it will happen without actively resisting temptation.

NEWSLETTER IDEA

Use these as a base for a parent newsletter, for youth-written articles, or for the parent section of the church newsletter.

How parents can equip to run.

But She Didn't Mean To!

As parents, we worry about the big three temptations: drugs, sex, and cheating. Though these are certainly threats, there are temptations that cause just as much damage:

- Gossip
- Ugly words to siblings
- Self-centeredness

In fact, if I were to pick the most dangerous temptation facing our teens, I'd pick selfishness.

Why? Because selfishness is at the root of all the other temptations. Selfish teens expect to feel good all the time; so when they don't, they turn to drugs.

Selfish teens expect to be the center of the universe; so when they feel a bit lonely, they wonder if sex will get someone to love them.

Selfish teens expect to have an easy time of making good grades and want the scholarships and attention that come with those grades. So they cheat to get the grade they claim to need.

Selfish teens assume their mood determines how everyone around them should behave. So if they're feeling cross, they say an ugly word to or about someone else. They find it reasonable to demand their way.

It's not that surprising really. We adults are too often just as selfish, expecting things to go our way and whining when they don't. Perhaps even more dangerous, we so hate for our teens to suffer that we protect them from any consequence or disappointment. Then they don't get used to the fact that life hurts sometimes. Because we've done all the hard work for them, they develop no coping strategies. They expect everything to be happy and don't accept it when it's not. Is it any wonder that they want to feel good all the time, have people dote on them constantly, and do what they feel like doing?

The diagnosis is easy; the cure is tougher.

What can we parents do to move our teens from self-centeredness to Christ-centered care and the happiness that follows such choices?

- *Realize it happens to everyone.* Rather than fret over your teen's selfish tendencies, remember that no one is born knowing how to reach outside of self. Babies are born totally self-centered, and it's our job as parents to teach our children-now-teens to move past that.

- *Start the teaching.* "You can't stay up all night and then sleep as late as you want. You'll have to be up by nine so you can help get the Saturday work done. Whatever time you need to get in bed to be well rested is the time you should choose."

- *Remember that you can get your teens to be good.* They say you can lead a teen to water but you can't make him drink. But if you just feed him enough salt, he'll drink. With a combination of rewards, punishments, motivations, and instruction, you really can enforce good behavior. Heart obedience will follow.

- *Realize that whatever your teen is used to is what your teen will expect.* If you pick up all his clothes, he'll keep dropping them. But if he must get them into the laundry basket to get them washed, he'll develop considerate habits.

- *Stop keeping your teen at the center of the universe.* If you pamper him, he'll expect to feel good all the time—and will eat, spend, do drugs, or do whatever he can to maintain that feeling. But if you honestly approach life as is—"Even when it's inconvenient, we have to do it"—he'll buck up and persist through the easy and hard of life.

- **Insist on kind words.** Getting along with parents and siblings is the main teaching ground for getting along with teachers, coworkers, bosses, and church members. You can tell a spoiled person by the way they treat people.

- **Be matter-of-fact rather than shaming.** Rather than, "How can you be such a pig about the bathroom!" say, "We need to make an agreement that gets both you and your sister ready for school on time. Ten minutes in the bathroom and then out you come. Then she'll have ten minutes. That's the selfless, family way to do things."

Prayer: Lord, please carve away at my selfishness while I mold my teenager into a selfless and caring human being. Help both my teen and me practice your Philippians 2:4 directive to "look not only to your own interests, but also to the interests of others."

E-MAIL IDEAS

Choose from these parent support ideas, tips and strategies especially for electronic transmission. (Remember: Don't create an E-mail Elite; print out and mail the messages to any parents who don't have E-mail).

We Christians too frequently have a skewed view of temptation. We wrongly believe that if we just get strong enough we can snuggle up to temptation and not get burned. In reality, the way to stay strong and to avoid temptation is to flee from it (1 Cor. 6:18, 10:14; 1 Tim. 6:11; 2 Tim. 2:22). Some examples:

Avoid—Don't go to parties where alcohol or drugs are served. You can't change the intent of that party, and you'll only put yourself into the pressure of doing as others do. (1 Cor. 6:18, 10:14)

Run—When a fight starts in the school hall, move away. Otherwise your temper may get the best of you, and you'll join right in. (1 Tim. 6:11; 2 Tim. 2:22)

Get Company—When a guy or girl gets too physical (especially if *you* are the guy or girl), stand up and walk back to where the people are. If your parents are upstairs, ask them to bring the chips. If you're off alone some-where, get on your cell phone and ask for a ride home. Some even find it helpful to sneeze repeatedly (Eccl. 4:12).

Resist—No matter how deliberately you avoid, run, and get company, you will be thrown smack in the face of temptation. Follow Jesus' example: quote Scripture, decipher half-truths, and discover when to hush and when to speak. Finally, just tell the devil to go away (Matt. 4:1–17; Luke 4:1–13).

And if you're sending the E-mail to a cell phone, send the single word only, with "Today's temptation resisting strategy is _____." Include one of the Bible verse references.

WHAT TEENAGERS WANT PARENTS TO KNOW

Choose from these questions that invite your teens to share with you anony-mous quotes, quips, and comments via E-mail or anonymous survey. Feel free to choose one question at a time as the "Question of the Week."

I'll combine your ideas, with no names or identifying details to distrib-ute to parents. Feel free to answer a question that's not here or to suggest another question for everyone to answer:

- How have your parents helped you be deliberately good so you're not accidentally bad?
- What are the top three temptations you face?
- What are your strategies for resisting those top three temptations?
- People tend to name drugs, sex, and cheating as the big youth temp-tations. But temptations like gossip, self-centeredness, and snobbish-ness are just as destructive. Explain.
- Name a rule your parents have that you use as an excuse to keep from a tempting behavior. What other rules might they add?
- Which of these is the most powerful temptation fighter and why:
  1. Run.
  2. Do something good in the place of a previous bad habit.
  3. Get a parent to help you fight the temptation.
- _____

TROUBLESHOOTING

What to do if a teen does not display the expected behavior.

Suppose you try to guide your teen past temptation, but he keeps on choosing to yield?

- Up the consequences. If your teen borrows the car without asking, especially after being restricted from driving, take his car keys or move the car to a place he cannot access it.
- Up the supervision. You may have to stay at home more often, stay in the room more often, even take turns with your spouse staying up all night. Developing your teen's sense of morality is worth it.
- Up the privileges for good behavior. When your teen stops selfish or dangerous actions, your teen will need something to put in their places. Insist on right behaviors and then reward with computer time, CDs, or whatever motivates your teen.

Bonus Idea

This idea is a word puzzle on ways to resist temptation.

Possible way to use: Duplicate this and challenge both parents and teenagers to bring it back to you completed. The answers are at the bottom of page 175. Ask, "Is there another temptation strategy that fits in four letters?" Publish these suggested strategies in an E-mail or newsletter.

Temptation Is No Puzzle

Though temptation can be confusing, there are at least four no-brainer solutions to it.

Change one letter per line to find them. The hints give you an example of that solution.

G __ __ __ if you're already doing the right thing and having a great time of it, you won't have time or energy to enjoy/get to know temptations.

__ __ __ __ When there's a good-looking guy whose character is shady, stay away from him.

Notice how telling the truth and treating people right brings true __ __ __ __dom and happiness. Sin only stresses.

__ __ __ __ Let yourself worry about the bad things that could happen (and usually do) if you choose to do, think, or say the ugly thing.

Here are the answers: *Glee, Flee, Free, Fret.*

CHAPTER 10

My Teen Wonders If There's a God

So answer spiritual questions and mold spiritual habits.

"My teen came home and asked me how I knew God was even real."

"What if we'd been born in another country? We might have a totally different religion. Don't you think religion is something people make up to make themselves feel safer?"

Questions like these can terrify parents. Isn't it wrong to question God? Where have we gone wrong? What if our teens turn their backs on God forever?

No, it's not wrong to question God, and questions about God's existence can show that we parents have done something extraordinarily right. Teens who question, trust that God is powerful enough to show Himself. And since God has already given evidences for His existence, there are answers to our teens' spiritual questions. The way to keep teens from turning away from God is to show them how to find answers to their questions. Some of the answers you'll know and can deliver. Others your teen will need to search out for himself or herself. Because real answers are available, we parents can let our honestly questioning teens search safely (Matt. 7:7).

Begin by affirming the question: "I'm so glad you care enough to question. Faith that is not questioned has no foundation."

Goal—This chapter guides parents to build with their teens foundations for faith so that faith in God can become their very own.

PARENT WORKSHOP

Draw from these ideas to lead a one-hour parent workshop.

1. Christians Ask Good Questions

You'll need for each parent a copy of the word search puzzle. Photocopy the puzzle, first enlarging it. Arrange chairs in two equal rows facing each other. If you have an odd number of parents, plan to participate yourself.

As parents enter, give each a copy of the word search puzzle and let them choose their own seat. The parent across from them becomes their partner to work together to find the ten questions teenagers ask about God. (Answers found on page 196)

```
W I L L G O D T A K E A W A Y M Y F U N D W C B A
L M K P L D B J K W D F D T M T J B P C D H F L W
W H A T I S H E A V E N L I K E D L M F K A T C H
H K D D F S W L D C P J T C M X D L K B M T W P Y
Y F T K M M G T X D P C T B L D L J W C B I K P C
W H A T I S G O D S W I L L P B M F C X W S P L A
O L K P D P P J D C M W T B X K L C Y T P G X K N
N C D O E S G O D R E A L L Y C A R E J W O J F T
T L L Y D K B F F B E T W C Y K X Q Q T X D F C W
G C J B K X W T X F H A B T H Q X J F H K L W X E
O W H Y D O E S G O D A L L O W B A D T H I N G S
D Q T H B W X H Q Z X B T H J Z W X H B X K H Z E
T Z C D D J F W F L V V W Z S S C D B X L E V F E
A S B K D C W F L V X J P S S V F B D C K V P S G
L L D V B C P C L S W W K J P C X R B R W R K S O
K D K P F B W I L L G O D G E T M E I F I M B A D
```

The questions are these:
Is God real?
Does God really care?
Why does God allow bad things?
What is God's will?
Why can't we see God?
Why won't God talk?
What is heaven like?
Will God get me if I'm bad?
What is God like?
Will God take away my fun?

Remind the parents sitting across from each other to help each other find the ten questions. When they find all ten, have that duo join an unfinished duo to work as a quartet. When all finish, point out:

We helped one another until all of us found the answers. That's what living as Christians is all about. We ask our questions and help one another find the answers God gives, to honor God well in daily life. Sometimes our teens ask questions like these. First assure them that questions show you trust God to have the answers. Second, assure your teen that there are answers. "Even if you have to keep asking the questions until the day you die, the answers are there. Some we'll know this side of heaven; some we'll know after we die. But it's never wrong to ask and ask and ask. The only time a question becomes bad is when you ask it to get out of doing something you already know."

Third, point your teen to sources of answers: the Bible, God's character, believers who are further down the road, reliable Christian books, and more. Assure your teen that you will help. Demonstrate how you have searched these sources.

Finally and surrounding all the other three, point your teens to the answer. "Honey, I understand some of the answer, but not all of it. The evil in this world is mostly due to human choices that affect innocent people like your friend. Other evil, like babies who are born with disabilities, seems to be due to the imperfection of this world. I wish God would instantly fix it. But God Himself will sustain us until we do get the answers. Let's lean on Him as our answer with a capital A until we can find the answers with lower case a's."

Discuss further with questions like these:

- **What other questions have you asked or heard a teenager ask?**
- **When our teenagers start asking questions, they are ready to take on faith as their own. How have you seen this happen?**
- **Why do expressing doubts and asking questions actually lead to deeper faith?**

 **Teaching Tip**

Why not just have parents list the questions their teens are asking? Because most parents carry a ton of worry that if their teens are asking questions, their teens don't have faith. We know this is not true, but not all parents know this. Even if they know intellectually that it is OK to ask questions, they emotionally worry that their teens aren't as spiritually mature as the other teens. The word search lets parents both experience and feel that questions are OK and good.

2. Sometimes Good Questions Are Still Scary

You'll need Bibles and graph paper with nice large squares.

What is your first reaction when your teenager asks a question about God or about faith?

Hear all reactions, mentioning why each one makes sense.

Using parents' comments, explain:

Say: **Sometimes we're proud when our teens ask questions. We like it that they take life seriously enough to understand how God guides it. At other times we are terrified! We wonder if it's wrong to question God or if we have let our teens down in some way. What if our teens turn their backs on God forever?**

Staying in the two rows, and with the same across-the-aisle partners, distribute graph paper and direct the pairs of parents to prepare a crossword grid of fears they have about their teens' questions. They can share answers with other parents as they work, including the placement of the questions on their grids. Starter fears include:

```
M Y T E E N M I G H T T U R N H I S B A C K O N G O D
A
Y           B
N E V E R F I N D A N S W E R S
E           T                                 I
V           T                                 W
E           E                                 O
R       H A R D T O A N S W E R Q U E S T I O N S
G           N                                 T
O           E                                 K
T           S                                 N
O           S                                 O
C                                             W
H                                             A
U                                             N
R                                             S
C L O S E S S E L F O F F                     W
H                                             E
                                              R
```

Say: **Naming our fears helps us fight them away.**

Call on a parent to read aloud 1 John 4:18.

Continue: **Because of this promise, we can keep our fears from inter-fering with our teens' need for answers. Too often parents or teachers force teens to hide their questions because of ways they respond. What might be some of these ways?**

Hear all parent suggestions, peppering in these samples as needed:

• *How can you ask such a thing?*

• *Don't you know it's wrong to question God?*

• *Your questions are way too hard; just believe!*

Explain that the problem with such responses is twofold:

1. It's not true; honest questions actually lead to deeper faith. God wel-comes questions.

2. Our teens then push their questions inside and suffer in lonely con-fusion. How much better to lay the questions on the table and find the answers together!

Call on a volunteer to read Matthew 7:7 as God's promise to guide us to answers.

To continue to assure parents that questions are good ways to grow in Christ, invite the group to name advantages to asking questions about God and faith.

Samples:

- *Questions about God's existence can show our teens want to know their faith is reliable.*
- *Teens who question trust that God is powerful enough to show Himself.*
- *Since God has already given evidences for His existence, He has provided answers to our teens' spiritual questions.*
- *The way to keep teens from turning away from God is to show them how to find answers.*
- *Because God has made real answers available, you can let your honestly questioning teen search safely.*
- *Questions keep youth from getting pulled into cults.*

We are sitting across from each other in two rows to illustrate two points. First, asking questions is not like a standoff, but like reaching out to the people in front of you and working together. Second, history is like a row of people who all ask similar questions. By asking people who have come before us, and people who go after us, we can share answers.

 # Adaptation for a Youth-Parent Meeting

If youth are present, invite them to make a grid of reasons they hesitate to ask questions. Reasons might include:

- I don't want to look unspiritual.
- Someone was horrified the last time I asked.
- I've been told we aren't supposed to question God.
- I worry that no one else asks this question.
- Or invite a teen who has questioned and found answers to tell about the process.
- Or invite a teen to tell how a book such as *Mere Christianity* by C. S. Lewis or *Your God Is Too Small* by J. B. Phillips helped them find answers.

3. But What If I Don't Know the Answers?

You'll need Bibles and a chalkboard or poster. Add numbers one to four.

Turn to a chalkboard and write the numbers one to four. Next to number one, write: "I'm so glad you care enough to question. Faith that is not questioned has no foundation."

Say: **As we affirm our teens' questions, they will bring their questions out into the open where we can find answers together. Then someone with false answers won't jump in to confuse our teenagers.**

Next to number two write: "Second, assure your teen that there are answers." Invite a volunteer to read Romans 1:19–20. Explain:

Say: **The most reassuring part of questions is that God gives the answers. God does not fear being questioned. Warn your teen to steer clear of any religious leader, group, belief, or practice that allows no questions. This happens frequently in cults. Fear of questions show the leader or religion has something to hide. You can ask God anything. The true God, true beliefs, and true practice will stand up under questioning.**

Explain further that even if we have to keep asking the questions until the day we die, the answers are there. Some we'll know this side of heaven; some we'll know after we die. But it's never wrong to ask and ask and ask. The only time a question becomes bad is when we ask it to get out of doing something we already know. Briefly explain that when Gideon laid out a fleece, he did not honor God. Gideon already knew God's instructions. When Thomas asked, Jesus gladly gave evidence. He did not condemn Thomas. Thomas then gladly affirmed Jesus as Lord.

Next to number three write: "Point your teen to sources of answers including the Bible, God's character, believers who are further down the road, reliable Christian books, and more." Invite parents to give several answers to:

Where do you go to find answers? What are some books that have helped you?

Jot these source titles near number three on your poster.

Next to number four write: "Point your teens to the answer, God Himself." Explain: **Some questions we can't fully answer this side of heaven. But God Himself will sustain us until we do get the answers. So lean on Him as your answer until you can find the answers.**

Invite a volunteer to read Revelation 21:3–4 as testimony of this.

To review and stress the value of questions, ask parents:

- **Why is it dangerous to believe in God without evidence?**
- **How does the evidence for Christianity lead to deeper faith?**
- **What do we do if we don't know the answers to a question our teenagers ask?**

Affirm the question and then search together.

4. Answers You Can Count On

You'll need Bibles. Duplicate and cut apart the seven evidences for God so each parent can have one. Then duplicate for each parent a copy of the seven evidences intact so parents can take home all seven.

Give each parent one of the following seven evidences in random order and challenge them to stand and find others with the same evidence. Then assure parents:

Say: **God has given us solid evidence for His existence. This evidence is more like evidence for friendship or love, realities that are powerfully true but not testable in a test tube. Together with those who have the same evidence, tell in your own words how your evidence points to the existence of God.**

If you have more than one parent for each evidence, prompt all parents to speak part of the presentation rather than one speak for all.

1. Nature—Nature is not random. It is orderly, consistent, and beautiful. Could this order have happened without a designer to plan it? Could this beauty have happened without a personal, caring Creator? No. A "big bang" would cause big destruction, not an orderly result. Explosions create chaos, not beauty. A personal Creator plans, designs, executes, and stays involved with His creation.

----

2. Human Individuality—All human faces have two eyes, a nose, and a mouth, but each one is unique. The uniqueness of each person points to a personal Creator who values individuals. If we were created by a neutral force, why aren't we all clones?

----

3. Sense of Right and Wrong—The fact that each person has a sense of right and wrong points to a moral Creator. Even people labeled as sociopaths have a sense of right or wrong when the action is against them. If there is no good God, and no personal Creator, where did a sense of right and wrong come from? Without God everything should be a matter of personal preference. But because God exists, even a serial murderer will admit that it is wrong to kill. He ignored his conscience and acted on his own plan.

----

4. The Presence of Love—How do you explain that human beings care about one another? Rocks and trees don't love, so why do people love? Where did love come from if not from a loving God who created us? Why do babies need their parents long after they are not physically dependent on them? Why do males and females want an exclusive relationship? Why are we lonely when we feel no connection with other people? Human ability to give and receive love shows that we are guided by more than instinct. It also shows that we are more than a random collection of atoms.

5. Yearning for Something More—It's not enough just to get up, go to school, do our chores, eat, earn money, and sleep. We want more. We want meaning, relationships, and purpose. Many call this yearning a God-shaped emptiness that only He can fill. Unless God fills this void, we can never find contentment. Serving God brings the purpose and meaning we seek. Matthew 6:33 is evidence that God must be first before family, friendships, school, and work can go well.

---

6. Jesus Christ—Jesus Christ is much more than another religious leader. He is unique because He is both totally God and totally human. The Jesus of history is God Himself. Jesus rose from death never to die again. Only God can do that. Jesus is God's ultimate revelation of Himself. He and only He died to show us how much God loves us. Through Jesus, God showed people what He is like. He became a human being so as Almighty God He could communicate with human beings.

---

7. The Bible—More than just another holy book, the Bible comes directly from God. The Bible tells us how God acted in the past, how to obey Him in the present, and how He will act in the future. It has more evidence for its reliability than other printed documents. These evidences include historical, archeological, scientific, and internal proofs. Second Timothy 3:16 describes the Bible as God-breathed and useful for teaching, rebuking, correcting, and training in righteousness.

Ask: **What other evidences has God given for Himself? What is your favorite Bible promise or description of God?**

Invite a volunteer to reread Romans 1:19–20.

Ask: **What do you like about a God who has revealed Himself?**

Give each parent a copy of all seven evidences.

What other evidences could we add for God's existence?

 **Time Note**

If time is almost over, skip step 5. If you have extra time, use step 5 to guide adults a step deeper in examining the evidences for God's existence.

5. But What About . . .

You'll need Bibles. Duplicate the seven arguments against God so each parent can have one. Consider duplicating for each parent a copy of the seven arguments intact so parents can take home ways to disprove all seven.

Say: **Even with strong evidences for God's existence, certain realities make our teens wonder. God's evidences overcome these arguments, but you must show your teens how.**

Once again give each parent an argument. Direct them to find others who have the same argument. Challenge the teams to counter the arguments with one or more of the seven evidences they have in their hands. Examples, in italics, follow each argument.

Argument 1—What about hurricanes, tornadoes, and earthquakes? Those aren't orderly or beautiful. A good God wouldn't include those in his creation.

Hurricanes, tornadoes, and earthquakes are distortions of God's goodness. They result from the Fall, as do illness and death. Paul described this as the groaning of creation in Romans 8:20–22. Even with hurricanes, tornadoes, and earthquakes, most of nature is still good and harmonious. One day nature will be redeemed.

Argument 2—Apes and other higher vertebrates also have unique personalities and do unique things. Perhaps individuality is part of evolution.

If animals evolved, why do each of the previous species still remain? Why didn't all of them change? No scientist has found an actual link between apes and humans or between any other two species. We have theorized based on similarities, but evolution remains a theory with no hard evidence. It's much more probable that we see humanlike behavior in apes just as we see it in our pets. The Bible clearly states that each species was created after its own kind (Gen. 1:21–25). This explains that though the order of creation matches the order of evolution, each species was created individually rather than blended into the other. One species did not evolve from another. God created each species. He then created humans in the image of God.

Argument 3—If God cares, why does He make some people more capable or beautiful than others? Why are there people with handicaps who did nothing to deserve or cause them? Why do cruel people not suffer at all?

When sin entered the world, disease, decay, sorrow, and death followed. Consequently we find genetic problems, handicaps, and other imperfections in this world. These problems are not God's design nor His perfect will. They are problems linked to this imperfect world. God cries when these things happen. Then He equips us to rise above obstacles until that day when all is as perfect as God meant it to be (Rev. 21:3–4).

Argument 4—Some cultures do terrible things like abandon crippled babies or value boy babies above girls. They don't seem to understand right and wrong.

Those mistakes don't excuse those who commit them. Some people may be confused about this, but they have definite rules of right and wrong in other areas. In every culture (including ours) there are people who do terrible wrongs. They can choose to recognize these wrongs and turn back to right.

Argument 5—Not everyone loves. Many people hate or selfishly use others. Why would God allow this?

If we have the ability to show love, we must also have the option of choosing hate. God will not force anyone to love Him or to love people. But He will help us love Him and love people when we choose to. For love to be real, it has to be free. Love must be voluntary if it is to be genuine.

Argument 6—Many people seem content with a nine-to-five routine. They don't think past it. They have no room for God in their lives.

Most likely we just don't see their struggles. Or they may have buried their discontent long ago. You may notice their yearning for more in their selfish indulgences. They don't see God because they choose to close themselves off from Him.

Argument 7—There are many religions and religious leaders. Who are we to say Jesus is the Son of God?

We don't have to say Jesus is God's Son; Jesus has already said it. He has also proven His divinity in His life, lifestyle, and death. No other human has risen from death, never to die again. Jesus came to establish a relationship with us, not just to give religious rules. He practiced what He preached. He showed us how to live. He lived by His own rules. He is God from birth.

Adaptation for a Youth-Parent Meeting

If youth are present, invite them to present the seven step-5 arguments while parents help them answer those arguments. Suggest that the students be humorously pushy and keep on arguing. This will bolster the parents' declarations of truth and help them be specific in presenting what is real. Rather than leave parents to flounder, whisper points as needed.

The Point

Make a copy of "The Point" on colored paper to give to parents.

Assure parents that they don't have to have all the answers to guide their teens to the answers. The main thing they need to do is to affirm the question. Then they and their teens can search together. Review the four steps to doing this, using your step-3 poster.

Give each parent a copy of "The Point," perhaps enclosed in a question mark, and then ask:

What is your favorite Bible promise that God will provide answers and help?

➤ The Point

Guide your teenagers to search out and discover the answers to their spiritual questions.

"Ask and it will be given to you; seek and you will find; knock and the door will be opened to you" (Matt. 7:7).

Because God is the answer, and because God generously shares answers, your teens can discover that a relationship with God is more than just wishful thinking. True faith is discovering what is, rather than decide on what you want to believe. Searching helps us discovering this. Real faith is reality based and bolstered by real evidences.

HOME DISCUSSION GUIDE

Send this page home with parents, mailing to any who were not able to attend, or mail to each parent a few days after the session as a follow-up prompter to practice the point.

The Point of our last parent meeting was to guide our teenagers to search out and discover the answers to their spiritual questions.

God has chosen to reveal Himself (Rom. 1:19–20). An unquestioned faith tends to be weak. Cults pull in many victims by insisting that the faithful do not question but simply believe. Real and solid belief has a foundation of standing up under all scrutiny. Jesus promised in the Sermon on the Mount, *"Ask and it will be given to you; seek and you will find; knock and the door will be opened to you"* (Matt. 7:7).

Because God is the answer, and because God generously shares answers, your teens can discover that a relationship with God is more than just wishful thinking. It is discovering what is, not what we just wish to be. It's reality-based and bolstered by real evidences.

Evidences for God's Existence

Cut apart the following evidences for God's existence and lay them out on your kitchen table. Invite your teens to take turns picking one and telling why it gives evidence for God's existence. Because you practiced these at the parent meeting, you can guide the discussion well.

1. Nature—Nature is not random. It is orderly, consistent, and beautiful. Could this order have happened without a designer to plan it? Could this beauty have happened without a personal, caring Creator? A "big bang" would cause big destruction, not an orderly result. Explosions create chaos, not beauty. Only a personal Creator brings beauty.

2. Human Individuality—Human faces have two eyes, a nose, and a mouth, but each face is unique. If we were created by a neutral force, why aren't we all clones? The uniqueness of each person points to a personal Creator who values individuals.

----

3. Sense of Right and Wrong—If there is no good God and no personal Creator, where did a sense of right and wrong come from? The fact that each person has a sense of right and wrong points to a moral Creator. Otherwise everything would be a matter of personal preference. Even people labeled as sociopaths have a sense of right or wrong when the action is against them. Even a serial murderer will admit that it is wrong to kill. He ignored his conscience and acted on his own sinful schemes.

----

4. The Presence of Love—How do you explain that human beings care about one another? Why do babies need their parents long after they are not physically dependent on them? Why do males and females want an exclusive relationship? Why are we lonely when we feel no connection with other people? Rocks and trees don't love, so why do people love? The human ability to give and receive love shows that we are guided by more than instinct. It also shows that we are more than a random collection of atoms.

----

5. Yearning for Something More—It's not enough just to get up, go to school, do our chores, eat, earn money, and sleep. We want more. We want meaning, relationships, and purpose. Many call this yearning a God-shaped emptiness that only He can fill. And unless God fills this void, we can never find contentment. Serving God brings the purpose and meaning we seek.

6. *Jesus Christ*—The person Jesus Christ is much more than another religious leader. The Jesus of history is God Himself. Jesus rose from death never to die again. Only God can do that. Jesus is God's ultimate revelation of Himself. Through Jesus, God showed people what He is like. He became a human being so Almighty God could communicate with human beings.

----

7. *The Bible*—More than just another holy book, the Bible comes directly from God. The Bible tells us how God acted in the past, how to obey Him in the present, and how He will act in the future. It has more evidence for its reliability than other printed documents. These evidences include historical, archeological, scientific, and internal proofs. Second Timothy 3:16 describes the Bible as God-breathed and useful for teaching, rebuking, correcting, and training in righteousness.

Discuss with your family:

- What do you like about worshiping a God who has given evidences for His existence?
- Why is true faith discovering what is, rather than deciding what you want to believe?

God does not fear being questioned. Urge your teens to steer clear of any religious leader, group, belief, or practice that allows no questions. Fear of questions show the leader or religion has something to hide. You can ask God anything. The true God, true beliefs, and true practice will stand up under questioning. Ask your teen: Why is it dangerous to believe in God without evidence? How does the evidence for Christianity lead to deeper faith?

NEWSLETTER IDEA

Use these as a base for a parent newsletter, for youth-written articles, or for the parent section of the church newsletter.

Rejoice When Your Teen Questions

Is it panic time when your teen comes home with questions about God? No, it's rejoicing time (Matt. 7:7). That rejoicing will become solid faith when you guide your teen toward good answers from reliable places.

Why Questions Are Good

1. Asking God questions shows you believe He can handle them.
2. Asking shows that you're ready to make faith your own.
3. God has the answers.
4. God is the answer.
5. Asking helps you know to obey. For example, if you ask, "Why do bad things happen to good people?" and you find that people do most of the bad things, you can choose to do good things. You also can help people through bad times by doing practical things for them.

When Questions Are Not Good

1. When the question is not sincere.
2. When you're asking to get out of doing something you already understand (the Gideon mistake in Judg. 6).
3. When you don't pursue the question to the end.
4. When you ask the question to escape God rather than to learn.
5. When you use the question as an excuse to turn your back on God. For example, you ask, "Why are there are so many hypocrites at church?" and you simply stop going to church. In that way the hypocrites take over, and your God-given service goes undone.

How to Turn a Not-So-Good Question into a Good One

1. Admit to yourself and to God that you're not being sincere.
2. Change your question to a genuine one.
3. Keep asking until you understand.
4. Talk with a parent or other honorable Christian and search your Bible to find hints that speak to your question.
5. Go ahead and obey what you do know even while you wait to understand what you don't know. For example, I may not know my spiritual gift, but I do know to love others as I love myself. So I won't abuse my brother.

E-MAIL IDEAS

Choose from these parent support ideas, tips and strategies especially for electronic transmission. (Remember: Don't create an E-mail Elite; print out and mail the messages to any parents who don't have E-mail).

Teenagers don't always ask aloud the questions they have about God and about life. Reasons they give include:

"The last time I asked, someone reacted with horror."

"I've been told we aren't supposed to question God."

"I don't want to look unspiritual."

"I worry that no one else asks this question."

Encourage your teens to ask aloud what they are asking inside by assuring them that asking questions shows they trust God to have the answers. (We ask the math whiz when we have a math question.)

You can invite your teen to ask more questions in these three ways:

1. Let your teen see you wonder and question and then search for the answer.
2. Let your teen see you continue to do the right thing even when you struggle.
3. Ask: "What kinds of things do you wonder about God and about Christianity? What do you wish you understood better?"

And if you're sending the E-mail to a cell phone, here's a short one: E-mail to your teen: Anytime you have a question about anything you can come to me with it.

WHAT TEENAGERS WANT PARENTS TO KNOW

Choose from these questions that invite your teens to share with you anonymous quotes, quips, and comments via E-mail or anonymous survey. Feel free to choose one question at a time as the "Question of the Week."

I'll combine your ideas with no names or identifying details to distribute to parents. Feel free to answer a question that's not here or to suggest another question for everyone to answer:

- What questions do you have about God?
- Who has shown you how to answer questions well? What did this person teach you?
- What questions do you have about church? Many times these questions have nothing to do with God. Explain.
- What answers have you already found about God, and how are you living the answers?
- What distinguishes Christianity from other religions?
- What can parents do to help teenagers answer questions?

TROUBLESHOOTING

Suggest these actions to implement when a teen does not display the expected behavior.

Suppose your teen becomes rebellious against church and all things spiritual?

- Just as you get him to school, get your teen to Bible study and church every Sunday. Then make certain he stays in class and worship even if you have to park outside the classroom and seat yourself within sight of him during worship. Only as he's at church can he make connections with other Christians.
- Pick a good church with a good youth Bible study. If you switch churches, switch as a family. Don't send your teen to another church without you.
- Repeat that asking questions is OK; bucking against God is not.
- Agree that questions make you angry with God, but most of the time another target deserves the anger. The accurate targets include the human who caused the problem, the disease, or the devil who prompted the evil.

Bonus Idea

This idea is a list of places to go for answers. Give multiple copies to parents so they can keep one as well as give one to their teens.

Possible way to use: Enlarge, print as a folded card, and recommend that parents keep it in their own billfolds or bureaus, and give one to their teens for the same purpose.

Places to Go for Answers
Where shall you and your teenagers ask, seek, and knock?

1. *The Bible*—This letter from God is verified by manuscript, historical, archaeological, scientific, and internal evidences. Rather than find one or two verses that speak to the question, get the whole picture, a total Bible view of the issue by looking at longer passages and full books. For example discovering how to grieve is addressed by such passages as Ecclesiastes 3:1–8; John 11:35–36; 1 Thessalonians 4:13–18; and Revelation 21:1–4.

---

2. *God's character*—This is the ultimate whole-Bible issue. Who is God? What is He like? What does He do? By understanding God's character, we discover that He doesn't hurt people or give them more trouble because they are "strong."
3. *Older believers*—Believers who have lived their faith over the years understand more about how God works and how to obey Him well. They have discovered what principles/sayings/approaches are flimsy and which ones stand the test of time. Find honorable believers who live out their faith rather than just talk. They more likely understand God's character.
4. *Books*—Classics such as *Mere Christianity* by C. S. Lewis and *Your God Is Too Small* by J. B. Phillips explore the questions many believers encounter. Newer books help too, as long as they harmonize with Scripture.

```
W I L L G O D T A K E A W A Y M Y F U N D W C B A
L M K P L D B J K W D F D T M T J B P C D H F L W
W H A T I S H E A V E N L I K E D L M F K A T C H
H K D D F S W L D C P J T C M X D L K B M T W P Y
Y F T K M M G T X D P C T B L D L J W C B I K P C
W H A T I S G O D S W I L L P B M F C X W S P L A
O L K P D P P J C M W T B X K L C Y T P G X K N
N C D O E S G O D R E A L L Y C A R E J W O J F T
T L L Y D K B F F B E T W C Y K X Q Q T X D F C W
G C J B K X W T X F H A B T H Q X J F H K L W X E
O W H Y D O E S G O D A L L O W B A D T H I N G S
D Q T H B W X H Q Z X B T H J Z W X H B X K H Z E
T Z C D D J F W F L V V W Z S S C D B X L E V F E
A S B K D C W F L V X J P S S V F B D C K V P S G
L L D V B C P C L S W W K J P C X R B R W R K S O
K D K P F B W I L L G O D G E T M E I F I M B A D
```

A Strategy for Ministering with Parents

A handful of ideas, cautions, and tips.

Parent meetings are tough to pull off:
- Kids don't want parents getting together to talk about them.
- Parents worry that their teen is the only one struggling.
- Some parents like whining more than taking action to help their teens.
- Parents of teenagers are even busier than their teenagers.

A few key actions can help with this:
- Institute a no put-down rule. "Here we treasure teenagers. Certainly we guide them. We teach them. We sand off rough edges. But we do all that at home. Publicly we declare their positives, loving them as we love ourselves in obedience to Jesus' command."
- Affirm gutsy parents who keep on parenting because parenting teenagers is a daily thing.
- Thank parents for the specific expressions of godly character they grow in their teenagers; keep a checklist until you've affirmed each teenager to each of his or her parents.
- Refuse to play into "My teen is giving me so much trouble." Instead prompt action with, "How can you equip your teen to master that situation?"
- Provide ministry through more than meetings including:
    - ✓ Home discussion guides
    - ✓ Newsletters

✓ E-mail messages
✓ A question of the week
✓ Record parenting tips and Bible promises on answering machines.
✓ Teens sharing anonymously with parents what they want parents to know
✓ Troubleshooting strategies
✓ Bonuses like idea cards, refrigerator magnets, and rules for fair fighting

Develop a true team stance through which you learn as much from parents as they learn from you.

You'll need more than a sentence at a meeting to show you respect parents as the experts and God as the authority. To demonstrate you want to learn as much from parents as they learn from you, check off each of these suggestions as you do them within the next six months. Be certain to invite input from all parents even if only a few respond.

☐ I send E-mail to invite ideas from all parents.
☐ I have called a parent for advice.
☐ I send letters or postcards to invite ideas from parents.
☐ I overview the youth calendar with parents before finalizing it.
☐ I have invited a parent to preview or review a program or an event.
☐ I have started an event or program due to wise parental input.
☐ I have changed a program or event due to wise parental input.
☐ I invite parental wisdom in writing newsletter clips/articles.
☐ I invite parental wisdom in choosing topics and listing youth needs for programming and ministry.
☐ I courageously listen to a quietly wise parent, even if a whiney one speaks louder.
☐ I hear both parents who agree with me and parents who do not agree with me.
☐ I use parents in the actual planning and implementing of ministry.
☐ I enlist parent advice before there are problems.
☐ I avoid a parent clique by inviting all parents to preview/ evaluate/give input, even those I've never heard back from, just on the chance that they might want to share this time.

☐   Another way I've teamed with parents to minister with youth is

_____.

Build a team approach between you and parents. This is the most important tip of all.

1. ***Trust parents' honorable judgment.*** For example, "Your after-Sunday-night-program meetings mean a tired teen all week, one who can't witness as well for Jesus because he's so weary. Could you put the meeting before your other Sunday programs?"

2. ***Call on parents as more than snack supper hosts/drivers.***
   - Invite them to give you feedback:
     - Each negative bookended with two positives.
     - Each positive named with a way to make it even better.
   - Call on their areas of expertise.
     - Enlist graphic designers to prepare your youth brochure.
     - Call on farmers to teach about the sower and the three soils.
     - Invite teachers to beef up your Bible study methodology.

Refuse to think of parents as someone else to whom you have to minister. Instead, see them as those with whom to minister.

Together you and parents equip youth to participate in God's kingdom.
- It's not limited to programming.
- It's working together to guide teenagers to participate as members of God's kingdom wherever they are.
- It's working together to implement strategies that equip teens to care for people the way God cares for them, to participate in this world according to God's plan.

Let us consider how we may spur one another on . . .
- toward love
- toward good deeds
- toward encouragement
- toward Christlikeness

(Heb. 10:24–25)

. . . by doing what only the church can do.

Write Your Own Session

A sample process by which to compose a parent meeting on any topic.

Want to get word to parents about a particular topic? Preparing a parent meeting on a topic not in this book?

Follow three basic strategies:

1. Write down what you want parents to know, do, or understand.
2. Put that information into several formats. You can get the word out in articles, in mailings, in E-mail messages, on posters, and more to whet appetites for the meeting and to help before and after the meeting.
3. Use the information to prepare your meeting.

Step 1: What Do You Want Parents to Know and Do?

Whether via meeting, E-mail, postcard, letters, church newsletter, parent newsletter, youth mailing, computer-generated projection in adult area, or any other strategy, first determine the information you want to spread. Think of it as good gossip.

Start with jotting down what you want parents to know/be blessed by/be equipped by/understand/act on. Write rapidly about your topic without worrying about grammar, spelling, or what's most important. Later you can sort it, reword it, and put it in the order you want. You also can decide later what to do with the information: whether to write an article, use as the basis for your meeting, or a combination of both. Here's a sample on the topic of emotions all run together to demonstrate that even your jot list can become an intro game for your meeting. Parents divide word from word to discover some key points about emotions:

YouthareemotionalYouthcanmanagetheiremotionsYouthneedparentsto
teachthemhowtomanageemotionsAngeroftenisasignofsomethingelsesuchas
fearorconflictbetweenwhatyourteendoesandwhatyourteenwishesshewas
doingAngeroftenmakessenseTellyourteenthatangerisgoodwhenitmotivatesy
ouoryourteentochangeawrongtoarightAngerunharnessedisdangerousHeart
hereasonsyourteenismadandsadandgladAgoodwaytogetteenstotalkabout
emotionsistoinviteorinsistthattheytellyouthreesentencesaboutitNomatterhow
youthfeeltheymustdotherightthingNomatterhowparentsfeeltheymustdothe
rightthingGoodnovelscanshowteenshowtomanageemotionsProvidestructure
inyourhomeforsafeexpressionofemotionsExpressyourownemotionswell.

Step 2: Put It in Several Formats

These samples use the information above.

An article for parents called "My Teen Won't Talk to Me."

Do you want to hear what your teenager feels and thinks, hopes and dreams? Great! Studies show repeatedly that the person teens most want to listen to them is a parent.

Depending on how things currently are in your home, it may take time to get your teen to open up. Begin by praying. God is the guide for good relationships. Then invite conversation when it is most comfortable for your teen, not for you:

- When she first arrives home—let her call you at work, or stop what you're doing if you're home.
- When he's falling asleep—problems loom big at night. Develop the habit of coming in a few minutes before lights out to say "I love you and I'm here for you. Anything left from today that you'd still like to say?"
- Whenever your teen talks—stop and listen.

A good way to talk about a tough topic is to insist that your teen tell you three sentences. "I don't have to know it all, but give me just three sentences." ("I don't want to talk about it" doesn't count as a sentence.)

Tip for the Week

Develop the habit of always telling your teen why what she said makes sense. It's a good way to show understanding.

Myth Defused

Myth—Now that my child is a teenager, I no longer have power over his friends. This one he's running with makes him combative and angry.

Truth—Your teen needs you more than ever to help him choose and grow friendships. An angry friend is not just an inconvenience; he can ruin your teen's life. Develop the habit of talking over strengths and weaknesses of each person, not in a critical way but with the goal of choosing friendships with whole and happy people. Open your home as a place your teen can bring friends. Thank your teen for the good friends your teen picks and grows close to. Talking about friends doesn't have to be an emotional battle but a choosing together who brings out the best in your teen and vice versa.

Question of the Week

What action works best in your home for getting your teen to talk about his or her feelings?

Then provide these to give parents more resources than you alone can provide:

- A book that might help
- A person who might know
- A parent who might teach me
- Invite the class of youth to give input. (Always call on all youth in a grade or department; don't pick a youth group elite because God has designed the church to be a body, not a hierarchy—Eph. 4:4–16.)

Step 3: Use the Information to Prepare Your Meetings

A good parent meeting involves parents in the topic the minute they walk in the door. You've noticed a different type of parent blender for each of the ten meetings in this book. Change the chairs, change the assignment, change the method, and in so doing keep your meetings always intriguing. A book such as *Youth Worker's Guide to Creative Bible Study* (B&H, ISBN 0-8054-1837-7) will spur your own ideas. It offers 350 methods, plus 32 ways to form teams and a dozen ways to group your chairs.

Once your parents are involved in the topic, go deeper and wider by studying Scripture and applying it to the topic. Vary your methods and approaches to let parents find and apply the truths for themselves.

You'll want about five steps in your meeting, the first an engaging opener and the last a memorable closure. The three in the middle are your deep Bible study and application. The ten sessions in this book offer sample approaches and use only a fraction of all the approaches available. They also list materials (*"You'll need . . ."*) and preparations (*"Do this . . ."*) for each type of approach. You'll want to make your own lists.

To give parents a take-along prompter, pick one key point based on the Bible passage you're studying and print it for parents to take home.

The Most Important Step

Remember that parents are the experts and God is the authority. You are simply the guide to link the two together.

Over Four Dozen Topics for Parent Meetings

Having trouble thinking of your next parent meeting or parent newsletter theme? Try these.

This alphabetical list of topics provides over four years of monthly parent meetings. Let it jump-start your own ideas based on the unique needs of your community.

Accountability or How to Affirm Your Teenagers

Brothers and Sisters or Bad Behavior and How to Manage It

Church Involvement or Conversing with Your Teens or Christlike Behavior in Teens and Parents

Disciplines of the Christian's Life or Death and Dying or Dating

Emotions or Eating Disorders or Evangelism

Friendships or Family Budgeting or Fruit of the Holy Spirit

Give Them Wings (Equipping for Adulthood)

Health or Homosexuality or Happy Home Habits

Independence or Idols or I Just Don't Know What to Do

Journaling or Junior Year

Keeping Your Sanity as a Parent and as a Teen through the Teen Years

Loving or Leadership

Money Management or Marriage Readiness

"No" Is Not a Dirty Word or Needs of Youth

Optimistic Attitude or Opening Doors of Maturity

Peer Pressure or Personality Types or Plain Old Fun with Your Teenager or Power

Quiet Time and Other Daily Disciplines

*R*ecreation or *R*espect or *R*unning Away or *R*esources

*S*chool or *S*ibling Relationships or *S*cholarships or *S*piritual Gifts or Service

*T*ime Management or *T*eaching Talking Skills or *T*emptation Fighting

*U*nderstanding Your Teenager without Excuses

*V*ictory over Problems

*W*isdom or *W*hat Are You Wearing?

*X*amine Your Attitudes and Those of Your Youth

Y and X Chromosomes—Guy/Girl Issues or Why? How to Handle Faith Questions

*Z*ealous and Energetic Parenting